Dave- Keep

Up the great

work

[signature]

23 Equity Crowdfunding Secrets to Raising Capital

23 Equity Crowdfunding Secrets to Raising Capital

JOBS Act Marketing

Craig Huey

Media Specialist

ISBN: 978-1-54393-434-2

To my beautiful bride Shelly, who has been by my side through thick and thin. She has been my gift from God, best friend, cheerleader and prayer warrior.

To my children; Asher, Julia, Caleb, Kelly and Cory, who have all seen and participated in the sacrifice necessary for success. For their continued love, understanding, encouragement and fortitude.

A special thanks to members of my team for making this book become a reality.

Caleb Huey; an expert of the benefits of equity crowdfunding who has joined me in panels, seminars, webinars, speeches and in private meetings. What Caleb brings to the table is true transformational wisdom that launches successful campaigns.

Kelsey Yarnell; an avid copywriter who has done the research and clarified and crafted a complex issue into readable, dynamic content. Without her skills and wisdom, this book would not have happened.

Finally, I thank God for directing my path, not just for my career but for my entire life. It is in Him whom I place my trust. (Proverbs 3:5,6)

The Equity Crowdfunding Revolution
Marketing to Investors to Raise Capital Under the JOBS Act

Raising capital as a private company without becoming a public company is now a reality.

Raising capital as a pre-IPO or mini IPO to fast track into becoming a public company…is now a reality.

The JOBS Act revolution will help create an economic boom in the United States…and your company can be part of it.

Eighty years of a discriminatory and unnecessary stranglehold on investors and private companies has ended… and now new opportunities have burst open for both groups.

A mutual win-win.

I wrote this book as a guide to show you how your company can raise capital by marketing to investors – a group I've been marketing to for more than 30 years, for which I've helped to raise over a billion dollars in assets.

I welcome your questions and trust this will equip you with the guidance you need to see dramatic growth, thanks to equity crowdfunding.

Craig A. Huey

Craig Huey, President
Creative Direct Marketing Group, Inc.
Nobody knows direct response and digital marketing better.

About Craig Huey and Caleb Huey

Craig Huey is publisher of the industry newsletter *Direct Marketing Update*, and President of Creative Direct Marketing Group, Inc., a full-service direct response advertising agency.

Craig has the distinction of being recognized as one of the nation's top direct response marketing experts. His insightful and on-target strategies have generated more investor subscribers, leads and sales than anyone else in the industry… and have helped companies raise more than $1 billion in assets.

Over the years, CDMG's marketing programs have garnered 87 major industry awards.

Caleb Huey is Vice President of Creative Strategy at Creative Direct Marketing Group. For more than 10 years, he has been on TV, spoken at conferences and helped provide investment marketers with new ways to expand and grow.

Caleb is a "JOBS Act" crowdfunding expert who has been helping companies worldwide launch, grow and dominate their markets.

Craig and Caleb have made millionaires out of entrepreneurs and helped million-dollar organizations skyrocket to even higher levels of success.

Clients have included:

Monaco, Real Writer, Humana, Starshop, 1-800-Contacts, Agora Publishing, Baby Lulu, Blanchard & Co, Brainy Baby, Chevron Oil, Chronomite, CompuSOURCE, Data Transmission Network, Day Focus Planners, Debt-Free Living, Dyansen Galleries, Educational Insights, Family Life Seminars, Forecasts & Strategies, Giltspur, Group 3 Electronics, Hooked on Phonics, Instant Office Freedom Alliance, Investment Seminars International, Jews for Jesus, Laser Eye Center, Lear Capital, Maranatha Music, Micro-Design Resources, Midwest Center for Stress & Anxiety, Mommie Helen's Bakery, Soldier's Angels, Spidell's Tax Service, Sterling Travel, Sun Chlorella, Supercircuits, Surf Control, The Hollywood Reporter, The Motley Fool, TheStreet.com, The Weather Channel, True Religion Jeans, Weight Watchers, Zacks ... and more than 200 others.

Table of Contents

Foreword

Across the United States, I have been giving marketing talks and seminars to raise capital under the JOBS Act in a revolutionary way. The response has been stunning. And the key to successfully raising capital is what is called "direct response marketing."

Direct response marketing has held me captive and mobilized my business for over four decades. Together, my team and my clients have raised over a billion dollars in capital for a variety of investment products and services ... winning 87 awards along the way.

My clients have trusted me with their marketing, advertising, growth and expansion. I am honored and eternally grateful to them.

One of my most exciting experiences throughout my career is helping to build, develop and grow companies from unknown startups into successful and profitable corporations.

Direct Response Marketing tools and techniques are my specialty. For years, companies have needed more capital. Now, under the JOBS Act, equity crowdfunding has emerged as a powerful way to be able to grow a business. The merging of marketing and raising capital is not just exciting; it's the catalyst for tremendous increase.

And I believe this will help create new business, innovations, jobs and wealth.

CHAPTER 1
What Is the JOBS Act?

On a sunny spring day in the White House Rose Garden, President Obama signed into law the "Jumpstart Our Business Startups" Act, also known as the JOBS Act. It was April 5th of 2012, and the business climate was about to undergo a massive change.[1]

The JOBS Act is an important, historic piece of legislation with an incredible impact on the potential for small businesses, startups, hedge funds, investment funds and even public companies to raise capital and attract new shareholders.

The JOBS Act changes how ideas are funded, giving entrepreneurs more access to the capital they need to grow their businesses … and gives investors incredible new opportunities available previously only to bankers, investment insiders and Wall Street investors.

In fact, the JOBS Act may be the most significant act in the past 80 years.

It is fueling new business growth, jobs and innovation.

For business owners and entrepreneurs, it's the fastest, least costly way to generate capital. For investors, it's a way to get in on the ground floor of a new business, or find unique opportunities for larger profit potential than ever before.

The JOBS Act could produce an economic boom of historic proportions.

Here's a summary of the JOBS Act's major, historic changes:

- The General Solicitation Ban on asking for money publicly for investment has been lifted. This was an 80-year-old ban that restricted you from advertising investment opportunities in your business.[2] Now, you can market your investment opportunity directly to the public.

- If a company wishes, a fast-track approach to becoming public is now available.
- A private company can have hundreds or even thousands of shareholders investing in the company.
- You can use an equity crowdfunding site to raise capital or advertise and market directly to the investor.

The gates of investor funding are opened. Now you can build your shareholder base, asking the investor to take a stake in your company with equity or debt. This kind of funding is open but still in its early phase, with changes and modifications expected by the SEC – under President Trump, a very friendly SEC.

In fact, I anticipate the full potential of the JOBS Act to be expanded when more deregulation occurs – removing unnecessary bureaucratic regulatory barriers.

Now, you don't need to go public (though a public company can raise funds under the JOBS Act) or work yourself too hard to get qualified investors.

You can use the capital you raise to:
- Expand your business
- Open new stores
- Market and advertise your product or service
- Perform research and development
- Hire new employees
- Purchase acquisitions
- Buy equipment
- Whatever you want…

The #1 Marketing Blunder that Many Equity Crowdfunding Companies Make

The JOBS Act has provided a historic opportunity for companies like you.

However, there's a dangerous mistake you can make as an equity crowdfunding company ... in fact, many equity crowdfunding campaigns fail.

Why?

They don't market their opportunity to active, long-term investors.

To have a successful equity crowdfunding campaign, you will need to know specific strategies and tactics to market your offer to these kinds of investors – and get the response you're looking for.

Your best prospects are the individuals who are most likely to respond to your offer and put capital into your business or venture because they have a history of investment.

In the following pages, you'll learn how to take advantage of this tremendous opportunity offered by the JOBS Act. I've provided you with a roadmap to create your own marketing program, with specific examples of actionable items, based upon 40 years of marketing to active, long-term investors.

CHAPTER 2
The Seeds of the JOBS Act:
The Crowdfunding Revolution

The JOBS Act is one of the most disruptive new laws in recent memory – a massive deregulation by the federal government.

It is transforming the way companies are able to expand, growing new jobs and opportunities for investment.

The JOBS Act reverses 80 years of government stranglehold on the economy, companies and investors. It has opened exciting new opportunities for the average investor to invest in a private company. But it's so much more than that.

- It's a way for private companies to become public, faster and cheaper.
- It allows private companies to raise funds without ever becoming public.
- It enables public companies to generate private capital.
- It also qualifies investment funds and hedge funds to raise capital.

It's revolutionary.

The Crowdfunding Revolution

The breakthroughs made possible by the JOBS Act really began with the advent of crowdfunding.

Crowdfunding is an extraordinary new way to raise capital, but the crowdfunding revolution was slow to start and awkward because of excessive government regulation.

That being said, crowdfunding has made incredible advances in helping organizations, individuals and businesses raise massive amounts of capital.

Stage One

How did the crowdfunding revolution get started?

First, it began with "reward" crowdfunding. Hundreds of millions of dollars have been raised from reward crowdfunding, which allows companies to raise capital from willing participants.[3]

With reward crowdfunding, all an individual gets in return for giving funds is a product or gift. This is not really investing – the company shares are not for sale. Participants basically contribute – they don't invest – to get T-shirts and other products. But still, the beginnings of reward crowdfunding proved there was a strong market for private investing.

Today, crowdfunding platforms like Kickstarter, IndieGogo and Gofundme continue to help companies raise capital with reward crowdfunding.

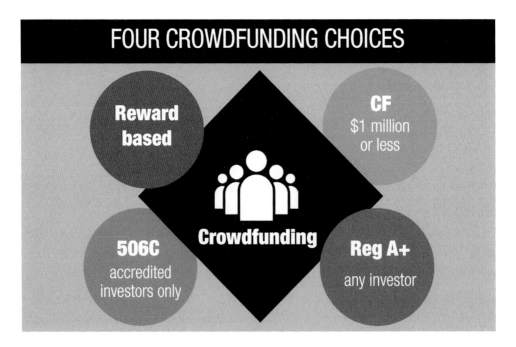

FOUR CROWDFUNDING CHOICES

Reward based

CF $1 million or less

Crowdfunding

506C accredited investors only

Reg A+ any investor

Stage Two

Then came early stage investing for the wealthy. About 20,000 accredited investors (individuals who meet specific financial qualifications) participated in early stage investing. These were professional and semi-professional investors who used crowdfunding sites to evaluate companies starting in 2011.[4]

This generated lots of excitement, but restricted vision and potential due to the limited number of investors.

Stage Three

The next major phase is what we have today…equity crowdfunding. I believe this is just the beginning of massive growth and expansion of equity crowdfunding.

It's hard to pick a date for the beginning of equity crowdfunding, as the SEC has been agonizingly slow in making changes and approvals to the JOBS Act. But if there's a day to remember, it is May 16, 2016, when the SEC greatly expanded the ability of companies to raise funds.

By some estimates, about $16 billion was raised in crowdfunding in 2014.[5] Around $34 billion was raised in 2015.[6] And in 2016, about $60 billion was raised through equity crowdfunding.[7]

While the figures for 2017 have not come out by this writing, it is estimated that by 2020, capital raised under crowdfunding will reach $90 billion.[8]

Most crowdfunding assets will be raised under Regulation A+, followed by Regulation 506C and finally, Regulation CF (which I'll explain in the following chapters).

The key to crowdfunding success is how well a company markets to the retail investor.

Do it right and you could exceed all expectations.

Do it wrong and it's a terrible loss of time and money.

This book gives you the roadmap to successfully market your investment opportunity to the active investor.

Three Major Categories for an Equity Crowdfunding Campaign

There are three major categories for the JOBS Act: Reg A+, Reg 506C and Reg CF.

In this chapter, I'll cover these categories, and what they require of participating companies.

I always recommend marketing in Category #1 under Reg A+, which I'll explain in a bit.

But first, let's look at the specific advantages and disadvantages of each category offered.

Category #1: Regulation A plus (or Reg A+)

Reg A+ is by far the best way to raise capital for both businesses and investors. The downside is that it requires more money and paperwork to be able to qualify with the SEC. This includes having a full audit.

Reg A+ has several key advantages:

- It enables you to raise funds from ANY investor, not just accredited investors.

THE THREE MAJOR CATEGORIES FOR THE JOBS ACT

Reg A+
any investor

506C
Accredited
Investors only

CF
$1 million
or less

- It enables you to raise up to $50 million dollars.

- It can act as a fast-track to becoming a public company, if you desire to do so.

I've worked with many companies that are raising capital with Reg A+. The most significant advantage of this approach is that it gives you the ability to market to the most active investors in America.

Companies have found Reg A+ to be a great way to generate capital. For example:

- VIRTUIX, a unique virtual reality product, raised $7.7 million from an estimated 1,600 investors.[9]

- Elio Motors raised more than $17 million.[10]

- Chicken Soup for the Soul Entertainment raised $30 million before listing on NASDAQ.[11]

- Adomani raised more than $14.4 million before listing on NASDAQ CM and shot up to over a billion-dollar market cap.[12]

- Celebrity chef Bobby Flay has filed under Reg A + to launch his new burger chain, which is slated to raise $15 million.[13]

By 2017, nearly 200 companies

had applied for Reg A+.[14]

By 2017, a total of 32 companies had successful Reg A+ transactions, raising a total of $396 million.[15]

Reg A+ companies can use either Tier 1 or Tier 2. One advantage of Tier 2 is that participating companies do not have to file from Blue Skies exemption on a state-to-state basis, saving them time and expense. The maximum offering under Tier 1 is $20,000. Under Tier 2, the maximum offering is $50,000.

Recent research showed that 32% of Tier 2 Reg A+ companies are in revenue mode, 15% are cash flow positive, and they average about 30 employees.[16]

Reg A+ campaigns are anticipated to collectively raise $50 billion per year by 2022.[17]

Let's take a look at two of the examples from the previous page that eventually went public after expanding under Reg A+.

1) Elio Motors was the first equity crowdfunding company to go public over-the-counter (OTC), after having raised more than $17 million from 6,600 investors under Reg A+. Just days after it listed its shares on the markets, Elio Motors' value soared past $1 billion.[18]

2) Adomani, which converts school buses and other fleets into zero-emission electric and hybrid vehicles, was the first company to move from a "pre-IPO" directly to the NASDAQ market.

Investors sent shares of Adomani up 2.6% after the manufacturer announced it had closed its Reg A+ common stock offerings, raising about $9.2 million in net proceeds.[19] The company, trading under the ticker symbol "ADOM," sold more than 2.5 million shares at $5 per share.[20]

We're going to see more and more companies becoming public in a "fast track" way and not through a traditional Initial Public Offering (IPO). They will already have raised capital

506C

Permitted Investor:
Accredited investors
only

Verification: Issuer
must verify that
investors are accredited

Dollar Limits: No limit
on amount raised; No
limit on how much each
investor can invest

Shareholder Numbers:
In general, any company
with more than 500
non-accredited
investors or more than
2,000 total investors
must become a full
"reporting company"
under the Exchange Act

**No SEC or State
Registration**

Marketing: Advertising
of any kind is allowed.
Internet, TV, radio,
leaflets dropped from
planes, anything

and generated shareholders, and will not have had to go through some of the time, costs and headaches involved with a traditional IPO.

For the companies who plan to go public, SEC legal filing costs average $127,000 for qualified offerings, and the SEC qualification averages 78 days. The fastest completion possible is 55 days.[21]

This is called the fast-track way to becoming public because it dramatically cuts time from becoming a public company the old-fashioned way. Audit costs average $29,000.[22]

If a company gets more than 500 un-accredited shareholders and around $10 million in assets, it must go public. Hopefully, this will soon be removed by Congress and the SEC.

Category #2: Regulation 506C

Raising capital under Regulation 506C requires far less regulatory oversight and expense than Reg A+. The main issue with Reg 506C is that you can only market to accredited investors.

Accredited investors are

wealthy individuals who meet certain financial requirements, but may not be actively looking for investment opportunities (For more details on accredited investors, go to Appendix A).

I've worked with many companies who are using Reg 506C to raise their funds from accredited investors. They can raise unlimited funds but have a cap of 2,000 investors.

Even with these restrictions, Reg 506C is still a potentially effective way to raise capital.

Category #3: Regulation CF

Regulation CF is a smaller category for equity crowdfunding deals. Under Reg CF, a company can raise $1 million and no more. I expect it shortly to be raised to $5 million.

This is a crowdfunding portal only, and those who market in this category are extremely restricted in how they can market and advertise.

For all three categories, the investor sets the minimum investment. For Reg CF, you typically make a minimum investment of $100 or more.

Here are two success stories of Reg CF campaigns:

- Beta Bionics is a bio-tech startup that has created a smart artificial pancreas for Type 1 Diabetes patients. It generated 775 investors with an average investment of $1,300 each.[23] The company is valued at about $100 million.[24]

- Hops and Grain is an Austin, Texas-based distillery company. It has hit its $1,000,000 cap.[25]

The bottom line is that the JOBS Act has opened up equity crowdfunding in a powerful way. It's transforming how investors invest. This metamorphosis is disruptive to the entire investment community. Average investors are now able to get in on the ground floor of a potentially huge increase in value for their investment, just like Wall Street insiders used to enjoy.

It's also a radical new way for companies to raise capital to grow, expand, invest for R&D, open retail outlets, increase manufacturing, fund marketing and more.

In the past, the three biggest stock exchanges – the DOW, S&P 500 and NASDAQ – dominated the investment market, but now that's all changing. Private companies are becoming accessible to investors, creating a fantastic way for companies to raise capital, and for investors to diversify their investment funds.

I believe with future equity crowdfunding, there will be no income or wealth restrictions. Anybody will be able to invest.

Equity crowdfunding will continue to change. The shackles will be taken off. The market will be allowed to function freely as it should, which would be to the benefit of everyone. Soon we will see what has been called liquidity for all: a liquid market of startup companies where anybody around the world can buy and sell shares.

But for now, we need to concentrate on how to reach the investor in order to generate shareholders.

Which filing category should you use?

I recommend Regulation A+ for most companies.

Again, Reg A+ gives you the enormous advantage of marketing and advertising to any investor, and raising a great amount of capital. Reg 506C and Reg CF are more limited... you'll be more restricted in who you can reach with your opportunity, and in some cases, how much you can raise and how many investors you can raise from.

In the next chapter, I'll show you the first step to effectively take advantage of this historic opportunity to fund your business and see profits soar.

CHAPTER 4
Four Critical Paths for Reaching the Investor: How to Raise Capital that is Targeted and Accountable

Radio and TV, even interviews, will not bring you investors.

Being on a crowdfunding platform and hoping investors will come just won't do it.

Even general advertising is a waste of time and money.

You must market, and market smart.

No company can raise millions of dollars from skeptical, cautious investors unless you use powerful, friendly persuasion – a targeted, accountable and aggressive outreach to your prospects.

In every element of the marketing campaign, your approach must use the foundations of direct response marketing, including direct response copy and a powerful offer.

To reach investors, I have laid out four paths of marketing/advertising choices to target for your business/investment opportunity. Targeted marketing will create results that don't rely on just using a crowdfunding platform and waiting for people to come to you.

Path #1: Highly Targeted Investors

This is the most efficient marketing strategy because you're communicating only to the most active investors, small-cap investors and startup stock investors. These are the individuals who are the most likely to invest capital in your business or venture. The target market is specific. You don't waste money and time on non-prospects.

For those choosing 506C, you must only market to accredited investors within this category to be compliant with the JOBS Act. But you can still use our Path #1 recommendations.

To effectively target these valuable investors, you'll want to use:

1) A direct response landing page designed specifically for the campaign
2) Direct mail sent to a target audience
3) Email sent to a target audience
4) Banner ads directed at a target audience
5) Facebook ads directed at a target audience
6) Pre-roll ads directed at a target audience
7) Retargeting with direct response banner and Facebook ads
8) Amazon ads directed at a targeted audience
9) Direct response video

All of these elements will be directed at your targeted audience among the most active investors, small-cap investors and startup stock investors.

Believe it or not, this multimedia integration works best when direct mail is the foundation. Direct mail is just what it sounds like: the direct delivery of advertising material to a prospect through postal mail.

Only with direct mail can you precisely and comprehensively preselect the most active individual investors or accredited investors in America.

I'll cover direct mail in greater detail in Chapter 10.

From these direct mail names, you can then deploy banner, Facebook, email and pre-roll ads to the same names you mail to.

This is called an integrated, multichannel campaign.

This type of campaign should produce the lowest cost per lead and the lowest cost per sale in generating new investors. In other words, it should be the most cost-effective way for you to produce thousands of new investors.

Let's look more closely at the nine key elements to a successfully integrated campaign with a highly targeted audience.

Campaign Element #1: Direct Response Landing Page

A special landing page is necessary to maximize response from the investor.

You do NOT want your prospect to go to your corporate website.

You want your prospect to go to a special landing page that matches the copy of your direct mail, email, Facebook ads and other advertising/marketing efforts.

You'll learn more about landing pages in Chapter 9.

Campaign Element #2: Direct Mail

Direct mail is the most efficient and effective way to target your ideal prospect. With direct mail, you're able to target only active or accredited investors. Mailing lists can identify your prospect by their investing history, special sectors they prefer, income and net worth.

No other media can achieve this in a comprehensive and confident marketing campaign.

The marketing cost for direct mail may be higher than some other media channels. But the lower cost per lead and cost per sale justify the extra upfront costs.

With direct mail, you have several strategic and tactical options, as you'll see in Chapter 10.

Campaign Element # 3: Email

Email lists allow you to target your investor audience, but

email alone usually does not produce the results you want.

Using the same names on the email list and the postal list, you will generate more leads at a lower cost per lead and lower cost per sale.

By combining email and direct mail, you will improve your ROI on both the email and direct mail campaign.

Chapter 11 details the most profitable strategy for email marketing.

Campaign Element #4: Banner Ads

Banner ads are online ads that appear on a variety of web pages.

Deploying banner ads to the same names from your direct mail and email lists increases response. See Chapter 12 for more information on banner ads.

Campaign Element #5: Facebook Ads

Just like banner ads, you should deploy Facebook ads to the same names used for direct mail.

Look-a-like audiences should also be used for Facebook. Learn more about Facebook ads in Chapter 13 and Look-a-like audiences in Chapter 16.

Campaign Element #6: Pre-roll Commercials

These are the commercials that appear before the videos you watch on YouTube or Fox Business, for example. Like all other elements, pre-roll commercials can be targeted to your direct mail list. See Chapter 14 for more on pre-rolls.

Campaign Element #7: Retargeting

Used by themselves, banner ads and Facebook ads are

okay for general investment marketing…but not great. Even with the right strategies and tactics, they may not produce the results you're looking for.

Add retargeting to the banner and Facebook ads and everything changes.

Retargeting is a powerful way to keep your name in front of your prospects, by "following" your prospects around the internet with specific banner ads and/or Facebook ads.

This powerful strategy is explained more in Chapter 15.

Campaign Element #8: Amazon Ads

This revolutionary new marketing tool can be used by crowdfunding companies to serve ads on Amazon to a highly targeted audience of investors.

Amazon will now provide powerful transactional data that gives you the ability to target prospects based on commercial transactions, rather than algorithms.

Learn more about Amazon ads in Chapter 17.

Campaign Element #9: Direct Response Video

Video can be highly effective when combined with your email, banner ads, retargeting and landing page. In fact, banner ads, Facebook ads, email and your landing page are much more effective when used with a video campaign – as you'll see in Chapter 18.

Path #2: Active Investors or Accredited Investors

With this approach, your marketing message is aimed at active investors or accredited investors.

This approach is less targeted and efficient than Path #1, because you end up wasting marketing money and creating a greater burden to qualify each prospect as an active or accredited investor.

In order to market effectively to accredited investors, I suggest adding the following marketing tactics to those described in Path #1:

Display Ads

Display ads in print and online magazines can powerfully complement your marketing campaign to the investor. High-end content providers are often city or regional magazines with a banner ad and email component. They target only high – net-worth prospects.

Magazines like *Money, Forbes, The Bull & Bear* and *Barron's* are your best platforms for display ads.

Display ads seldom produce enough response to justify a campaign, without an integrated marketing approach described in Path #1.

And they will not be as targeted, so you probably will be wasting finite resources on marketing.

Direct Response Television

I started my career more than 30 years ago with TV and I've created more than 400 commercials and 13 infomercials. I believe in the power of TV commercials and infomercials. They can be an extremely effective way to spread your message.

But they do not reach enough of your target audience.

Most of your audience – even those watching a financial television station – will not be qualified to invest in your opportunity. But a test on Fox Business, CNBC, Bloomberg and a few others will recruit some of the active or accredited investors you want.

Almost all financial TV commercials are aimed at the general investor. If you choose this approach, test 30- and 60-second commercials and consider a 30-minute infomercial.

TV should also be combined with the tactics described for Path #1.

Path #3: Active Investors and Accredited Investors, with Some Non-Accredited Investors and Infrequent Investors

Path #3 is less targeted. Unfortunately, some of your audience doesn't qualify for a 506C investment because they are not accredited investors. Some invest only in mutual funds or with a financial advisor.

If you choose Path #3, I recommend using the marketing elements laid out in both Path #1 and Path #2.

Path #4: Every Potential Investor

If you choose to market to every potential investor – that is, everyone – a very small percentage of the total marketing audience includes your target prospects. Most of those receiving your marketing message are not active or accredited investors.

Here are strategies you can use for Path #4:

Direct Response Radio

Radio is inexpensive and can be powerful – including a 30-minute radio infomercial. You can even target financial stations, all-news and talk-radio stations and Christian programs. These produce the best results. For those using 506C, there will be some accredited investors – but the clear majority are not.

Paid Search

Paid search is inexpensive. But it's difficult to reach the right investor with paid search, especially accredited investors. This could be a small portion of a campaign, but not as effective as those strategies described in Path #1.

Twitter

A limited Twitter campaign based on direct mail names can be used.

And a limited search to your target market can be done. Unfortunately, it's unlikely to add much value or response to your campaign.

Most of you reading these pages will want to start their equity crowdfunding campaign with the media outlined in Path #1, focusing on a highly targeted audience of active investors, small-cap investors and startup investors.

Further details described in Path #2 – Display ads, paid search and Path #4 – TV and radio, can be found on my website, https://cdmginc.com.

In the following pages, I'll unpack powerful marketing strategies that will generate quality investor leads at the lowest cost per lead/cost per sale possible.

These strategies are proven and time-tested…and rely on the power of direct response marketing.

CHAPTER 5

How to Raise Capital Directly from Investors with an Integrated and Multichannel Marketing Campaign

This is an historic opportunity for you. For the first time, you can directly reach investors to raise capital with an equity crowdfunding campaign.

Your marketing efforts can fall flat, wasting your time and money…or catapult you to success.

If you want to get a high response to your unique investment opportunity, you must use an integrated and multichannel marketing approach in your campaign.

This is the only kind of campaign that will help you to raise the capital you need to see your business take off.

You may be wondering:

What is integrated marketing?

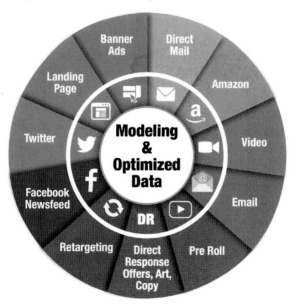

It's when your:

- Direct mail
- Email
- Banner ads
- Facebook ads
- Pre-roll commercials
- And Amazon ads

…All go to the same prospect names.

With this approach, active investors see the same opportunity advertised in their email inboxes, on their Facebook newsfeeds, before videos they watch on YouTube (pre-roll commercials) and anywhere else they may go on the internet.

Then, they receive a direct mail package advertising the same offer.

They're hooked.

I recommend integrated marketing because:

- It doesn't result in a waste of your efforts, time or resources, like image-based advertising can.
- Integrated marketing is highly targeted to prospects that will respond to your offer.
- It is scientific and accountable. With integrated marketing, you'll be able to measure and test results.

And finally, an integrated marketing campaign is a proven strategy to produce a powerful increase in response of shareholder leads and sales.

Integrated marketing directly to the investor allows you to generate more investor leads and more shareholders than ever before.

For my equity crowdfunding clients, I create an integrated and multichannel marketing campaign based on the opposite page.

As you can see, the campaign has different components.

INTEGRATED & MULTICHANNEL
MARKETING CAMPAIGN

NEWSALOG

LANDING PAGE

BANNER ADS

MAGALOG

FACEBOOK

PRE-ROLL VIDEO

EMAIL BLASTS

DIRECT MAIL

Integrated marketing may look complicated, but by using the following six steps, you'll be able to harness this powerful tactic to generate a great response.

Step 1: Use targeted data modeling and custom lists.

The first step to creating an integrated marketing campaign is to know how to target your ideal prospects. **Here are two primary ways that I help clients to reach active investors:**

Targeted Data Modeling

With this strategy, I create a precise and accurate replica of the ideal prospect – the individual who is most likely to invest in your company.

I do this by data modeling, which is critical in today's marketing world.

Using data modeling and prospecting, you'll be able to target only those investors who are most likely to respond to your offer and generate capital for you.

Using this powerful tool, I can create a custom list (Read more about custom lists in Chapter 6).

I can also profile and create a look-a-like audience that will further enhance your marketing efforts (Read more about look-a-like audiences in Chapter 16).

Data modeling provides you with postal names, email addresses and data that can be used for different marketing channels.

You may also use "direct response" investor names, those who respond to offers such as investment newsletters and magazines.

Custom Lists

You should also target prospects using your own lists.

By identifying investors among your existing customer or prospective customer lists, you will be able to target new prospects and generate leads.

This is an effective strategy because you know that these prospects are already interested in your product and brand.

With a powerful database of ideal prospects gathered from data modeling and your existing customers or leads, now you'll move forward in deploying your marketing materials.

Step 2: Create a landing page specifically for your investment opportunity.

All other components of your campaign will match the landing page in messaging and graphics. You'll drive traffic to your landing page through Facebook ads, banner ads, pre-roll ads, email and ads on Amazon. Plus, you'll retarget prospects who have visited your landing page and left before responding to your offer.

Step 3: Create and send a direct mail campaign.

Direct mail could be your most important part of generating new investors in your company or new venture.

It may seem Old School, but direct mail is still very effective in getting a high response.

There are several powerful options to generating an investor lead from direct mail, including a traditional direct mail package, a magalog, a newsalog, a bookalog, a 3-D package or a videolog. I'll cover these options in greater detail in Chapter 10.

A traditional mailing package includes a strong direct response copy letter, response device, lift note and value-added piece.

Step 4: Create an email campaign.

You should not use email campaigns on their own, but they can complement your integrated campaign by driving more traffic to your landing page.

Step 5: Retarget your prospects with banner ads, Facebook ads, Amazon ads and pre-roll commercials.

Whether on Google, Amazon, Facebook, YouTube or another platform, retargeting will be a powerful part of your strategy to increase lead generation.

Target the same names on your postal list with these ads, and you'll see response skyrocket. This part of the integrated campaign amplifies your effectiveness.

Step 6: Follow up with a conversion series and follow-up kit.

Next, you'll need a conversion series for prospects who turn into leads. For example, someone who responds to an ad online may receive a series of six to 12 emails, and one or two postal letters. This may include an email to prospects in November and January, and direct mail to prospects in December and February.

An integrated and multichannel campaign uses the same names for mail, email, banner ads, Facebook ads and pre-roll videos, so that you'll get maximum return on your marketing efforts – and succeed in raising the capital you need for your business or venture.

CHAPTER 6
Custom Lists: The Power of Your Database and Data Modeling

If your crowdfunding campaign has great copy….

An amazing offer….

A powerful landing page…

And matching Facebook ads, banner ads, email marketing and all of the necessary elements…

…but it's not targeted to the right prospects, it will fall flat.

In order to successfully market your offer to the right investors – and motivate them to respond – you'll need a refined, targeted marketing strategy for your integrated campaign. And one of the keys to developing a marketing strategy that succeeds is a custom list.

What is a custom list?

A custom list is a record of contacts that can be created from your customer file, the information you've already collected for your business or venture.

For equity crowdfunding campaigns, I use a customer file and identify who the investors are. Then I collect the postal addresses, emails and phone numbers of those investors and create a custom list.

You can use this custom list for Facebook advertising, Google, pre-roll videos on YouTube and other media to market the investment opportunity directly to your customer base. Because they know and love you already, they are more likely to invest in your venture and partner with you.

Using a custom list in your integrated campaign will increase individual investment and powerfully boost response. The results of this strategy can be so powerful that you are able to raise the capital you need from your database alone.

A second method for creating a custom list is to use a third party for data modeling, which will provide you with a custom audience of "perfect prospects."

It works like this:

Large database modeling companies record thousands of data points of transactional data, such as what a person has purchased over the past 6 months, one year or more; how they make purchases; their income and net worth; and more. Behavioral scientists are then able to "clone" the perfect prospect from this information.

Take a look at the graphic on the opposite page for an example of what kinds of transactional data are used in data modeling.

By gathering these different pieces of data – purchase history, income, donation history and other lifestyle demographics – data modeling can produce prospects that are the most likely to respond to your unique investment opportunity.

This is a powerful strategy for any marketer.

Custom lists are foundational to your campaign. They help ensure that you are targeting the right prospects with your integrated, multichannel campaign to the investor.

Data Modeling Transactional Breakthrough – The Perfect Prospect

- $350k per year income

  Net worth $5 Mil

  Used Direct Response

- Travel Magazine susbcriber since 2013

- Moved to Portland from California in August, 2015

- Spent $150 on denim jeans Size 12 May 7, 2017

- email: mhatter@comcast.net HHI: $100k

- Spent $300 on global items in 2016

- Spent $2,000 on home furnishings using Amex card within past 6 months

- Participates in monthly wine club. Orders selections online.

- Spent $70 on organic cotton sweat shirt, size 12 Nov. 18, 2016

- Megan Hattersley 2241 Seaport Dr. Portland, OR 97202 503-555-1234

- Donated $750 to animal welfare organizations during 2015

31

CHAPTER 7
Powerful Direct Response Copy Secrets for Marketing to the Investor

So far, I've laid out the different categories for equity crowdfunding marketing (I recommend Regulation A+).

You've also learned:

- The marketing paths you can take (I recommend Path #1)
- Elements of a successful integrated and multichannel campaign
- And steps to take to target this campaign to the investor.

You might think you're ready to go – to dive deeper into the details and learn how you can create and implement your own successful marketing campaign.

But hold on just a minute.

Before launching into specifics, it's key that you know the principles of direct response marketing.

You may create and deploy all elements of a successful marketing campaign…but get a very low return on your blood, sweat and tears if the content of your campaign falls flat.

The hallmarks of effective marketing are not beautiful aesthetics and clever writing. Effective marketing is never measured by what seems to look or sound good. It's measured by its rate of success.

Here's the bottom line: Effective marketing will motivate your prospect to pick up the phone and call your toll-free number, or go to your website and enter a credit card number.

So, what's going to drive your prospects to respond to your investment offer?

The Foundation of Successful Marketing: Direct Response Copywriting

More than beautiful graphics or short, cute copy, direct response copywriting will motivate your prospects to make an investment in your business.

Direct response copy is a unique, conversational style of copy that turns features into benefits. It develops credibility and reality in your advertising campaign.

In more than 30 years of writing marketing materials aimed at investors, I have developed some critical "rules" of direct response copywriting that should always be followed for increased response.

These time-tested strategies and tactics should be applied to every aspect of your integrated campaign: landing page, direct mail, email, banner ads, Facebook ads, pre-roll video, email and more.

Here are the 7 foundations to writing effective direct response copy:

1. Choose only direct response copy in all of your efforts.

At best, image-oriented ads help an audience feel good about your product or service, but not make a purchase.

Not only that, traditional advertising copy will kill your campaign.

Likewise, journalistic copy will depress response.

Good direct response copy is easy to recognize because your toll-free phone number is ringing more, your landing page is generating more leads and your crowdfunding platform is attracting new shareholders.

2. Direct response copy succeeds because it's based in science.

Most advertising agencies create art: beautiful design with clever copy. But if you want to get new shareholders, pretty art is only a small part of the battle.

Direct response marketing is based on the science of what makes advertising effective and why. Using tried-and-true rules, direct response copy will:

- Grab the attention of your prospect.
- Powerfully position your company and product in your prospect's mind.
- Identify your unique selling proposition (USP).
- Overcome your prospect's skepticism and objections.
- Create a "branding" effect that will help you gain market share.
- Motivate your prospect to respond immediately.
- Follow time-tested copy rules that work.

It's easy to see how mastering the science behind direct response copy gives your marketing materials the power to rapidly grow your investor shareholder base and dramatically increase your capital.

3. Direct response copy begins with you.

Direct response copy doesn't necessarily begin with a clever idea. It begins with "you." A good direct response copywriter will:

- Discover what's unique about your product or service and relate it to the "you" orientation of the prospect.
- Decide exactly how your investor prospects will benefit.
- Create a specific, clear theme for the prospect.
- Develop a personal, one-on-one communication.
- Reveal your unique selling proposition (USP) to your

prospect.

What's your unique selling proposition (USP)? It's what sets apart your investment opportunity from the rest...so prospects can't help but respond to your unique offer.

If you use direct response strategies, your prospects will clearly understand how your offer meets their needs and desires. Your prospects become your investors because they see what's in it for them.

4. Long copy almost always works better than short copy.

It might seem counterintuitive, but long copy almost always works better than short copy.

Take a look at this five-way test, shown at the right. This test was conducted to compare results using several different sizes of brochures, sales letters and a self-mailer.

This five-way test clearly demonstrates two important facts. The first is that a letter is one of the most important marketing materials you can invest in. The second important fact? As

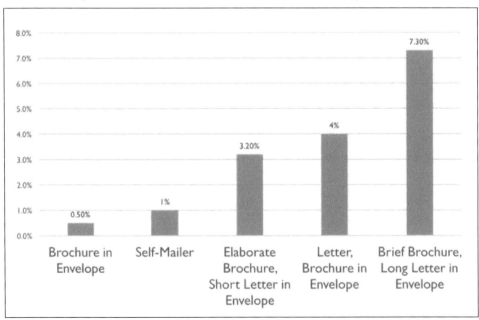

you can see from the test results, response to a long letter can significantly outpull response to a short letter.

Generating high-quality investor leads requires copy that is long enough to properly tell your story to a skeptical audience.

Your marketing deserves a sales letter, landing page, video and other media that:

- Pack an emotional wallop
- Show your prospects what's unique about you
- Explain why your investment opportunity will benefit them more than competitors' offers will
- Overcome their objections

Involving your readers and telling them exactly what you want them to do might take more than one or two pages of copy.

Lead copy should be shorter than sales copy that's asking for a sale. Also, the more you're asking for – especially $5,000 or more – or the more complicated your opportunity is to understand, the longer the copy needs to be.

As you can see from the chart on the previous page, long copy produces a higher response.

5. Direct response copy is a better return on your investment.

For decades, direct marketers using direct response copy have:

- Compiled the response rate to tens of thousands of emails, web ads, paid search, direct mail packages, radio spots and television commercials...
- Compared marketing copy and strategies with the quantity and quality of responses...
- Discovered which strategies and tactics were hugely successful, which were moderately successful and which

were devastating failures…

- Analyzed exactly why successful marketing strategies and techniques earned their companies millions of dollars in investors' money and why some didn't…
- And validated their discoveries through solid accountability, testing again and again.

Over the years, I have developed a knowledge base of copy strategies and techniques that work, as well as when they work and why, which I'll share with you on the following pages.

6. Writing great copy requires mastery of direct marketing strategies and techniques.

Your image-based advertising agency wants you to believe that no one can write sales copy like their clever copywriters. Don't believe them.

Even great writers don't necessarily write great copy. More than perfect prose or even perfect grammar, direct response copy will convince an investor to respond to your offer.

Direct response marketing is persuasive word engineering that relies on a set of foundational rules.

Break the rules and bad things happen.

Here are 40 rules for direct response copy that I use for a successful marketing campaign to the investor. Keep these principles in mind when creating all of your marketing efforts – direct mail, email, TV commercials, your landing page, video script, banner ads and anything else you may use – and you'll see great response.

Rule #1 *Remember to keep the first sentence short.*

Your reader will form an instant impression of your offer by reading the first sentence. If it's short and easy to read, chances are better that he or she will read on. But if it's slow, long or too complex, the reader might abandon it.

Rule #2   ***Another important rule is to make sure your intentions are clear.***

You may tease a reader on the outer envelope or headline of your landing page, but don't make your prospect read five pages to find out what you're selling. Remember, you have their attention at the opening – so don't be afraid to "fire your biggest gun" at that point.

Rule #3   ***Use specifics to strengthen your copy.***

Don't just write that your investment opportunity is unique. Tell the reader why, and use concrete examples.

Rule #4   ***Use specifics in your testimonials.***

For a health supplement, don't use, "Your vitamin is terrific. I feel great." Instead use, "I tried your vitamin…so far, I feel more energetic and focused. I'm sleeping better and I feel less anxious." Give your readers "meat," not generalizations.

Rule #5   ***Make sure what you provide is exciting to the reader.***

Sometimes what's exciting and important to you isn't interesting to the prospect. So, you need to key in on his or her needs and concerns, not yours.

Rule #6   ***Avoid the passive voice.***

Isolate all phrases telling what you'll do for the person. Then make sure to revise a passive voice to an active voice. Don't write, "The kit will be forwarded to you immediately." Instead, simply write, "I'll send you your kit now."

Rule #7   ***Remember that benefits outsell descriptions.***

Increasing "you-benefit" copy and minimizing

mechanical descriptions means better response. You won't sell a car by describing the type of safety glass or the gauge of steel, but a buyer will respond if you emphasize benefits: great handling, increased gas mileage, high resale value, performance, clean lines, etc.

Rule #8   *Another rule is to zero in on reader action.*

Your objective is to make the prospect say, "Yes, I'll invest!" If he or she doesn't act positively, then the only thing you've succeeded in is keeping your name alive as a reminder. Give readers the answers to their questions. Don't keep them guessing.

Also, don't forget to get the reader's head nodding in agreement. Keep him or her reading by maintaining the "yes" mood.

Rule #9   *Craft sentences so they're short and easy to read.*

Rule #10   *Avoid big words when shorter words are available.*

Rule #11   *Carve long paragraphs into several short ones.*

Rule #12   *Indent and use white space to its advantage.*

Rule #13   *Select hot words such as new, now, easy, introducing and save.*

Rule #14   *Vary paragraph lengths, but never write extremely long paragraphs.*

Rule #15   *Make sentences and paragraphs flow with natural transitions.*

Rule #16   *Occasionally insert a paragraph that consists of just a word or two, or a single sentence.*

Rule #17   *Use color for subheads, bullets and*

indentations.

Rule #18 *Avoid bureaucratic talk. Don't assume they all know the lingo.*

Rule #19 *Don't choose odd words that will pull readers' attention away from the sales message.*

Rule #20 *Weed out clichés and jargon.*

Rule #21 *Avoid too many commas and semicolons.*

They'll slow your readers down.

Rule #22 *Steer clear of new language.*

Words such as slang words and phrases may jar or confuse readers with meanings they may not know.

Rule #23 *Omit words that convey doubt or uncertainty:*

"I think," "It appears," "It seems," "You might find."

Rule #24 *Write in a language that's "you," not "I" oriented.*

- "You'll gain" (not "I provide")
- "You'll discover" (not "I'll show you")
- "You'll get a free" (not "I'll give you")

Rule #25 *Write in an active voice.*

"You'll get your free book," not "The free book will be forwarded to you."

Rule #26 *Use the present tense:*

"Invest now and you'll get a free bonus."

Rule #27 *Write to one person, from one person.*

Rule #28 *Don't brag – let the facts brag for you.*

Rule #29 *Pepper copy with scientifically proven power words:*

Own, Get, Control, Take, Care, Seize, Capture, Enjoy, Try, Grab.

Rule #30 *Use exclamation points, but sparingly!*

Rule #31 *Don't use asterisks (*).*

Rule #32 *Use ellipses (. . .) instead of dashes (–).*

Rule #33 *Avoid exaggerated claims.*

They will destroy your credibility. Superlatives are counterproductive. To claim that your service or product is the best in the world is automatically ignored by the reader and casts doubt on your entire presentation.

On the other hand, when you are specific and use actual testimonials, you gain credibility. Let others verify your facts and greatness, and let details and specifics reinforce your claims.

Rule #34 *Avoid complicated words.*

Simple words are powerful words. Legendary copywriter John Caples once said, "The headline of an ad for an automobile repair kit was, 'How to repair cars.' The headline was changed to, 'How to fix cars.' The second headline pulled 20% more replies."

Rule #35 *Have you eliminated all references to "I think" or "our company believes"?*

Remember, your prospects don't care about what you think, they only care about what they need.

Rule #36 *Do your materials anticipate and answer your prospect's questions?*

Write your copy as if you were face to face with your prospects and anticipating their questions.

Rule #37 *Do your materials anticipate and answer your prospect's objections?*

An objection is often a question. One way to turn a potential negative into an advantage is with a question-and-answer format.

Rule #38 *Can you relate your product or service to items in the news?*

Be careful to make sure it is timely and relevant to your product and its benefits.

Rule #39 *Have you defined your unique selling proposition (USP)?*

Do it at the start and reinforce it in the middle and at the end. This is what sets you apart – make sure it weaves through your entire message.

Rule #40 *Do your materials position your company as an authority with a solution to your target's worst problem?*

Make it clear that you are the obvious resource to meet your prospect's needs.

Your equity crowdfunding campaign absolutely requires using direct response copywriting that follows the rules.

When you build each piece of your campaign on the foundations of direct response copy, you're helping to ensure that you catch the attention of investors and motivate them to respond.

CHAPTER 8
Your Offer: Critical to Your Success

Like direct response copy, an irresistible offer is absolutely critical to the success of your campaign to the investor.

Your landing page, banner ads, emails and other marketing materials should entice your prospects with an opportunity that's difficult to resist.

If you're unsure of what an offer is, it's not what you're getting but what the prospect gets.

Remember, the investor is only human, like you or me. They are only interested in their own needs. They are not interested in making a philanthropic contribution to your company. They are interested in what they will get out of responding to your offer and investing in your venture.

What's more, your prospects are not sitting by their mailboxes, inboxes or televisions waiting to find out what you have to offer.

They must be engaged in conversation and enticed. And the best way to do this is to give them something that they perceive to be in their self-interest.

Something valuable. Something objective. Something that creates high interest.

Depending on your business or approach, think creatively about what you can offer potential investors as incentives to partner with you.

One of my equity crowdfunding clients is Starshop, a mobile shopping app that taps into celebrity trends. For their campaign, investors had the opportunity to participate in special events that tie into the company's product line.

This not only caught the interest of investors, it motivated them to respond to an offer that promised so much more than a financial opportunity.

Starshop's offer included entry to a New Year's Eve Party in Times Square with celebrities, DJs, full bar and a chance to dance the night away.

Another perk was a VIP suite at Coachella, a popular music and arts festival in Indio, California.

The offer also included entry to the Grammy's After-Party in Los Angeles at the Staples Center, where investors could mingle with the Who's Who of the music industry.

As if that wasn't enough, they were given the opportunity to go to a movie premiere in Los Angeles and New York with the full red-carpet treatment.

No traditional stock could make such an enticing offer.

Lastly, Starshop's offer included three special reports for the investor.

If there's an activity or special service that can be attached to your investment offer to increase interest, your campaign will attract greater attention – and capital.

The Power of Value-Added Marketing

Another way to boost your offer and create additional curiosity is to use the principle of value-added marketing in your equity crowdfunding campaign.

Value-added marketing is adding a gift or piece that educates and informs the prospect.

These types of pieces can include special reports, checklists or other informational items.

Value-added marketing can help elevate your offer and ensure the success of your campaign to raise funds in the following four ways:

1. **A value-added component will help get your envelope (or email) opened.**

When you offer something of value to the investor, they are more likely to open your envelope or email. Value-added pieces generate curiosity and interest in what you have to say…and offer.

2. **Value-added components help create the relationships you need with investors.**

Value-added pieces create a sense of trust, helping you to generate more leads and sales. They will motivate investors to put funds into your business or venture.

3. **Value-added components can totally change the tone of your direct mail piece.**

Value-added components change the tone of your direct mail piece by communicating that you don't just want your prospect's money, you want to help them. Value-added marketing will ultimately change their perception that you're there to take from them – a value-added component says that you're there to give.

4. **There is a great deal of variety of value added-components.**

One powerful value-added piece that I often create is a "kit." A "kit" can include useful information for the prospect in the form of special reports.

For a real estate-related offer, I created two special reports that the prospect would find valuable, worth reading and even worth keeping. The names of these reports were:

• *Secrets to Lower-Risk, Higher-Yield Investing*

• The Ultimate Guide to Profitably Investing in Real Estate

I branded these two reports as the Income Investor Profit Kit.

Ultimately, they helped motivate prospects to make a decision to respond to our client's offer, and helped massively boost response.

If you decide to create special reports, it's critical to give these editorial reports powerful titles that offer prospects highly relevant and useful insights or information.

The special report(s) might be two pages long – or 10 pages, or 20. They might even be 50 or 100 pages. They could be formatted as a PowerPoint presentation. Special reports can also be videos or downloads.

A kit can include a variety of different valuable informational pieces, but also a piece that helps explain why your offer is exciting.

To the right, see an "Investors Toolkit" I created for my client Allegiancy, a real-estate investment platform.

If done right, a value-added piece will give you a quality lead that will convert into an investor.

What you offer to the investor is absolutely critical to your success. Think

creatively about "perks" you can add to your offer, and how you can use value-added pieces to increase your success and the overall value of your equity crowdfunding campaign.

CHAPTER 9
The Foundation: Direct Response Landing Page

By now, you've learned two critical keys for your marketing campaign to the investor.

1. Direct response copy will win far more investors than image-based advertising or cute, clever copy.

2. A powerful offer is critical to the success of your campaign.

With these two components in mind, you are ready to develop a powerful marketing campaign to the investor.

A targeted, effective integrated marketing campaign begins with a landing page.

A fatal mistake in your equity crowdfunding campaign would be to use your own corporate website as the URL/website in the marketing program.

Most corporate websites have multiple purposes with different products and messages. When prospects arrive at a corporate website or homepage, they have many choices to make and directions to take. Plus, they are likely to have multiple messages and navigation bars – what I call navigation distractions that depress response.

And corporate sites don't have a focused call-to-action (CTA). The sales message is lost, usually muffled by distractions that kill response – losing leads, time and money.

In fact, most corporate websites are anti-marketing sites that present an idea that the investor prospect could not get excited about.

That's why the landing page is so important. A good landing page does not have navigation distractions. The landing page presents a single message that is clear and simple. It has a focused call-to-action (CTA) and drives the prospect to respond.

And, the landing page has copy and art that are compatible with the marketing materials, nothing else.

To an ad agency or graphic web designer, a landing page like this can look pretty boring. But for the investor prospect, it's what helps generate high response...and ultimately, investment capital for your business venture.

Here's an example (on the right-hand page) of a landing page I developed for my client Allegiancy, with the call-to-action (CTA) in the upper right-hand corner:

Here are five critical rules to creating an effective landing page for marketing to the investor:

1. Use direct response copy.

As I discussed in detail in Chapter 7, you must use direct response copy in every component of your marketing campaign...including the landing page.

One key to a successful landing page is to use powerful direct response copy to talk about your unique investment opportunity.

Direct response copy reinforces the offer that is in your mailing package, banner ads, emails and other marketing materials.

The landing page will also have longer copy about your offer than you would see on a corporate website, with the specific objective of motivating your prospect to pick up the phone to call and discover your new opportunity.

The copy on your landing page should speak directly to prospects ("you"), telling them why and how this offer can benefit them (For a full list of direct response copy rules, go to Chapter 7).

2. Show a clear call-to-action (CTA).

Remember, your landing page has one clear purpose: to

drive the investor to respond to your offer. That's your call-to-action (CTA), and it should be presented clearly.

The call-to-action (CTA) should be made clear on top of the landing page, and can be repeated multiple times throughout the page.

3. Retargeting powerfully boosts response.

Retargeting uses cookies on your landing page to "follow" your prospects around the web with digital ads, including banner ads and Facebook ads. This is a critical part of your marketing program that will increase response and drive prospects back to the landing page.

I'll cover retargeting in greater detail in Chapter 15.

4. Your landing page should have a video.

Video adds a powerful element to your landing page. Video is a unique marketing element that can create drama and deliver a message powerfully to the prospect.

When investors visit your landing page, they should immediately see a video.

For more information on video, go to Chapter 18.

5. Use direct response art.

Just like your copy, your graphics should invite your prospects to respond. Graphics should reinforce your big idea and not create unnecessary distractions.

Using these five rules to create your landing page, you'll lay a powerful foundation for the rest of your integrated marketing campaign…where you'll motivate the investor to respond and convert prospects to leads.

CHAPTER 10

Direct Mail: Specifically Targeting Your Audience to Generate High-Quality Investor Leads and Shareholders

Your landing page, banner ads, Facebook ads, Amazon ads and email are all valuable media to targeting your audience.

However, your #1 media to reach the investor with your opportunity is through direct mail.

Yes, it may sound Old School…but direct mail remains extremely effective in generating high-quality leads that will convert into investors.

Direct mail targets a specific list of investors with a traditional mailing package that is tailored to your offer.

No other component of marketing can target your prospect quite as specifically as direct mail.

I've overseen the mailing of over a billion pieces that have helped our clients dramatically expand their customer base and boost their revenue, sometimes growing from small companies into multi-million dollar businesses.

I also run a list management and brokerage company, InfoMat. One of the services that InfoMat provides is to identify and provide targeted mailing lists to marketers.

With more than three decades of expertise in this field, I've developed and executed proven strategies that can help ensure your success in your direct mail campaign.

Here are the seven critical keys to success in direct mail:

1. **The right mailing list** targets only the most active and likely investors with the best postal mailing list filters. It's a major reason direct mail can be so much

more effective than online marketing. I can help you with this critical step, by identifying and using the right postal lists for your campaign.

2. **The right direct mail format** effectively and powerfully communicates your offer. With a variety of formats, including a magalog, envelope and bookalog, you need to make the right choice for your campaign. I'll explain these different formats in a bit.

3. **The right direct response copy** is the most important and overlooked difference between success and failure. Use only direct response copy in your direct mail and see a massive response.

4. **The right offer** is a key to success. Your offer must entice the prospect to respond.

5. **The right landing page** is critical. Without it, your response will crash. Your direct mail package will drive your prospect to your landing page. If your landing page doesn't follow the principles outlined in Chapter 9, you're not going to get the response you're looking for.

6. **The right follow up with leads** ensures smart conversion. This step is essential, no matter how good your business opportunity is. You must follow up with leads using additional marketing.

7. **The right analysis** helps you to improve your campaign. You need to always know your cost per lead/cost per sale. This is scientific advertising. Analyze the results of your direct mail to help ensure you are marketing effectively.

Done right, direct mail will generate a lower cost per lead and lower cost per sale than any other medium.

One of the reasons direct mail is effective is because you can target your audience with specific mailing lists of proven, active, self-directed investors. Other kinds of media lack this precision.

Let's take a closer look at the first two keys, which are postal mailing lists and direct mail formats.

Direct Mail KEY #1: Investor Postal Mailing Lists

Fortunately for the equity crowdfunding marketer, investors are well-defined and identified in postal mailing lists. This will allow you to target your campaign at the right audience of prospects and get a great response.

Let's look at the three important mailing list options you can use to create a highly targeted and effective campaign aimed at the investor:

Option 1 – Direct Response Investors

Direct response investors are proven responders to investment campaigns. Having mailed to millions of these investors during the last 30 years, I know these direct response marketing lists inside and out...which produce the best response and which to avoid.

One of the keys to using the best direct response list of investors is to go to investment newsletter subscribers. These are people who have paid $100 or more for an investment newsletter. They are the best performing lists.

If you're using direct mail, you will want to go to those people that have responded to direct mail, not those who have ordered online. Direct mail responsiveness is key criterion for the success of a campaign.

And, I always look at R.F.M:

Relevance.

The more recent the names, the better the response.

Frequency.

The more they respond to different offers, the better the name.

Monetary.

The more they have paid, the better the investor's response will be.

These are predictors of how well a campaign will work.

With every campaign using direct mail, I analyze which lists are producing the most response, to what type of offer and promotion. This critical database of response helps us to avoid mistakes and ensures that we use the very best lists.

Option 2 – Data Modeling

I also use data modeled names for targeting active, direct mail responsive investors.

Data modeling can be used to generate names of the "perfect prospects" who will respond to your investment opportunity. These names are gathered by assessing massive amounts of transactional data, collected by database modeling companies (for more on data modeling, go to Chapter 6).

Modeled data will generate a much higher response than non-modeled data.

Data modeling dramatically enlarges your universe of prospects and increases response.

Option 3 – Accredited Investors

If you are marketing under Regulation 506C, you are restricted to accredited investors. Here's how I successfully market to this audience with a targeted postal list.

Under Reg 506C, a campaign to an accredited investor means targeting a person based on his or her income or net

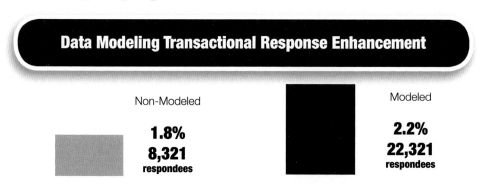

Data Modeling Transactional Response Enhancement

Non-Modeled

1.8%
8,321
respondees

Modeled

2.2%
22,321
respondees

worth. These are investors who are financially sophisticated, and believed to have less need for the protection provided by regulatory disclosure filings.

The following charts should give you an idea of the demographics of accredited investors in the United States.

For accredited investors who make more than $200K a year and are direct mail responsive…

Direct-Mail Responsive

Household Age	$200,000 - $249,999	Target Income $250,000 or More	Total
18-24 years old	1,622	552	2,174
25-34 years old	87,843	22,633	110,476
35-44 years old	427,336	172,764	600,100
45-54 years old	644,344	294,096	938,440
55-64 years old	463,672	170,039	633,711
65-74 years old	106,780	20,282	127,062
75+ years old	11,463	1,375	12,838
COLUMN TOTALS	1,743,060	681,741	2,424,801

For accredited investors who make more than $200K a year and don't respond to mail, or who are non-direct mail responsive…

Non-Direct Mail Responsive

Household Age	$200,000 - $249,999	Target Income $250,000 or More	Total
18-24 years old	145	9	154
25-34 years old	4,361	295	4,656
35-44 years old	15,777	1,078	16,855
45-54 years old	4,497	275	4,772
55-64 years old	369	17	386
65-74 years old	50	3	53
75+ years old	13	7	20
COLUMN TOTALS	25,212	1,684	26,896

Accredited investors can also be selected by net worth...

Net-Worth $1 million+

Household Age	Net worth $1,000,000+	Total
18-24 years old	2,411	2,411
25-34 years old	62,659	62,659
35-44 years old	511,102	511,102
45-54 years old	1,682,220	1,682,220
55-64 years old	2,786,397	2,786,397
65-74 years old	2,130,973	2,130,973
75+ years old	1,062,192	1,062,192
COLUMN TOTALS	8,237,954	8,237,954

Non-Direct Mail Responsive

Household Age	Net worth $1,000,000+
18-24 years old	1,006
25-34 years old	19,828
35-44 years old	195,882
45-54 years old	309,953
55-64 years old	404,546
65-74 years old	330,664
75+ years old	128,842
COLUMN TOTALS	1,390,721

You can make different types of selections from the accredited investors shown in the charts to better refine your targeting.

Here are examples of list segmentations where you can select more targeted data for a direct mail campaign:

- Male or female
- Living in a home or an apartment
- Geographic area – region, state, even local ZIP codes
- Income levels or net worth levels

Likelihood to respond to mail (known as direct mail responsive)

- Have an investment interest
- Show self-direction in making investments
- Like sports, gardening, travel, music and other psychographic variables

When selected carefully, these test segments help you to identify your most responsive leads.

Direct Mail KEY #2: The Mailing Piece – Format Options

A variety of direct mail formats can be used for a successful direct mail program. Here's an overview of the types of formats that can help you to create a powerful and effective campaign to the investor.

- **Traditional direct mail package.** This is a mailing package with a letter, lift note and response device inside an envelope.

- **Magalog.** A magalog looks and feels like a magazine but it's actually a direct response sales piece, crafted to generate interest and response in your product or service.

- **Newsalog.** Like magalogs, this is a unique direct mail format that can help dramatically raise response from investor prospects.

- **Bookalog.** A bookalog is a book that acts as an informational and advertorial piece to the investor.

- **Three-dimensional (3-D) package.** If you're doing a highly select campaign to a small audience of fewer than 10,000, I might recommend doing a three-dimensional piece.

- **Videolog.** This is high-tech direct mail at its best for an audience under 15,000.

Traditional Direct Mail Package

A traditional direct mail package is a powerful way to generate leads and sales. For the investor, it is one the most popular and successful formats you can use.

Traditional direct mail, if done right, can generate high-quality leads for your investment offer. I recommend direct mail if your offer is clear and easy to understand.

If your offer is more complicated, then I would highly recommend using the magalog, bookalog or a three-dimensional piece described on the following pages.

The traditional direct mail package consists of the following components:

Envelope

You might be inclined to ignore the envelope, but this is one of the most crucial pieces of your direct mail package. Why? A powerful envelope has one purpose: to get the investor to open it.

The lead generation campaign starting point of a traditional campaign is the direct mail envelope. The purpose of the envelope is to get it opened by your prospect.

If the envelope doesn't immediately catch the attention of the recipient, it will fail to be opened and your direct mail package will go wasted on a potential investor.

A powerful envelope can be a handwritten or a personally typed envelope, with high-quality personalization. I use a special machine that will "handwrite" using a pen.

Or your envelope can be address-filled by a computer, which is more commonly used.

Copy on the envelope – called teaser copy – will usually produce better response than a blank envelope.

That being said, I always test to see what will perform better in the marketplace. Take a look at the following examples of envelopes I've used in different marketing campaigns to the investor:

The first example shows an envelope that I produced for a company that marketed an investment opportunity in rare gold coins.

On the next example, notice that the name and address appear to be handwritten. This is an example of an envelope with machine-generated "handwriting." This can be an extremely effective method of getting your envelope opened.

Notice the "handwritten" request below the name and address on the example on the previous page. This detail can make the difference between a direct mail package that is responded to, and a package that is completely ignored.

Here is an envelope with teaser copy that immediately defines the unique selling proposition (USP) of the investment offer: "The banker's secret to potentially making...7%-10% yearly returns...paid to you monthly."

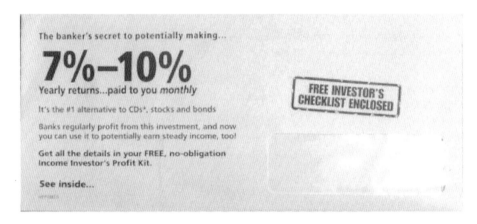

Letter

The most important component of a traditional direct mail package is a direct response sales letter. To generate the highest number of leads, a letter should be between two and eight pages long. Most lead-generation letters are four pages long.

The sales letter should include your unique selling proposition (USP), follow a clear and consistent theme, use persuasive direct copy and communicate your valuable offer. Here are five keys to creating an effective sales letter:

1. **Remember to keep the first sentence short.** Your reader will form an instant impression of your landing page, email or direct mail by reading the first sentence.

If it's short and easy to read, chances are better that they'll read on, but if it's slow, long, or too complex, they might abandon it.

2. **Watch your spacing in the letter.** For the sake of improved readability, single-space the letter and double-space between paragraphs. Most people find this style the easiest to read.

3. **Another important rule is to make sure that your intentions are clear.** You may tease a reader on the outer envelope or subject line, but don't make him read five pages to find out what you're selling. Remember, at the letter's opening you have his attention – so don't be afraid to "fire your biggest gun" at that point.

4. **Make sure your principal sales story is feasible**. Don't use an episode that's not believable. A prospect respects probability, but will reject improbability.

5. **Check to see if the components of your mailing package reinforce each other.** If you have a letter, brochure and lift letter or flyer, don't just repeat the same copy – include references in the letter to "see the brochure for full details." The brochure could include excerpted articles or more benefits.

An effective sales letter will follow the principles of direct response copy: use the active voice ("you"), use specifics and stress the benefits of this opportunity to the investor.

Lift Note

The lift note is a small letter inside the envelope, folded and signed by a credible signer who is not included on the main letter. This piece should not be overlooked, and can be a powerful component of your direct response mail package to the investor. The lift note gives a different perspective or reiterates the unique selling proposition (USP) of your investment opportunity.

The response device, or order form, is key to the success of a direct mail package because it gives the prospect the way to act on your offer.

One of the primary reasons some direct mail pieces bring in sub-par results is that the response device fails to follow tested and proven direct response rules.

The response device is separate from the letter itself. It can be a variety of sizes, but I recommend 8.5" x 11" or 8.5" x 14".

Here are four elements your response device must have:

1. **A clear call-to-action (CTA).** The response device is your chance to clearly spell out your offer, guarantee, discount premiums and the most important benefits – all in one spot. Clearly outline what the investor will receive by responding to your offer and why he or she simply cannot wait.

2. **Easy instructions.** Investors must be told exactly how to fill out your order form. If it is not easy to do, they will lose interest and you will lose the sale.

3. **Professional artwork.** Remember, your prospect will judge your product or service based on the quality of your response device.

4. **A Positive Acceptance Statement.** This powerful copy technique engages the investor and reinforces how he or she will benefit from your product. For example, an investment newsletter I created for a client said:

YES! I want more opportunities to be on the winning side of today's market. I'd love to add to my profits with your Wall Street Stock Forecaster picks that could bring returns of 100% to 300% or more.

Please begin my no-risk subscription to the only source of your huge safe-profit strategies, Wall Street Stock Forecaster, for the term I've selected below.

Simply saying 'Check this box for a one-year subscription' will do nothing to help you make the sale.

Using the key elements shown, you'll be able to create a direct mail package that gets a great response from investors.

There are, however, additional direct mail formats you can use to effectively market your investment opportunity. Below, I've outlined five other powerful and unique direct mail formats that you can use to set your offer apart from the crowd.

Magalogs: Infomercial in Print

The magalog is a powerful alternative to envelope mailings. It looks like and feels like a magazine, but it's actually an infomercial in print.

Here is an example of a magalog I created for my client Starshop, to the right.

Inside, I described cutting-edge investment trends in an informational format that the prospect would consider very useful.

The magalog, or magazine sales format, produces outstanding results for both consumer and business marketers. It's been especially popular in marketing to investors since I first pioneered the format in the 1990's.

My clients who market investment newsletters to their prospects use this format to create curiosity and generate a high response. On the next page see two additional examples of magalog covers that I've created for equity crowdfunding clients.

The magalog usually produces a higher response than a traditional mailing package.

If your product or service needs more explanation, images, graphs or pictures than can be easily included in a traditional direct mail package, the magalog may be the most effective choice for you.

Magalogs are valuable, informational and useful… and they produce amazing results.

The magalog provides a refreshing alternative to the sameness of the traditional direct mail package and has a longer life span and a greater "pass-along" value.

Unlike a traditional catalog, the magalog is not used to sell a variety of products or investments. It focuses on one product, with a variety of editorial features that highlight the investment opportunity.

One of these editorial features is the "sidebar." Sidebars are smaller articles that usually focus on one point or benefit, and then end with a specific reader call-to-action (CTA) to respond.

Covers should be informational. Adding page numbers on the cover helps to "tease" the reader inside.

Using bulleted copy lets the prospect know what topics will be revealed in the magalog. These bullets are similar to teaser copy in a traditional direct mail piece, in that they promise substantial information and value.

The back cover should also have more bulleted statements outlining the articles in the magalog.

What you say on pages 2 and 3 is critical and can mean success or failure. Page 2 generally contains a letter from the company president stating the purpose of the magalog, a table of contents or sometimes, the beginning of the lead article.

Page 3 starts the main article.

Most magalog formats are 16, 20, 24, 28 or 32 pages long, since printers find it most convenient to print in sets of four or eight. Usually, magalogs with page counts in multiples of eight will be the least expensive.

For equity crowdfunding marketing, I recommend 16-20 pages for lead generation. Obviously, the response, or call-to-action (CTA), form is one of the most important components of the magalog. The form should take up the last one or two pages.

In order to make the magalog look more upscale and reputable, four-color is recommended throughout.

Successful magalogs use powerful direct response copy and art – following, not breaking, the rules is critical to success.

Newsalogs: Counterintuitive, Yet Very Effective

Newsalogs are similar to magalogs, except they look and feel like a newspaper – but like magalogs, they are marketing pieces in disguise.

Newspapers may be in decline, but newsalogs are powerful pieces that will help raise your response rate.

This unique format should also follow the rules of direct response copy, and is best for those with an investment opportunity that may require more explanation.

I've seen this breakthrough format in direct mail create a 20-30% increase in response for multiple clients.

Bookalogs: A Tried-and-True Strategy for Investment Offers

Bookalogs are not new, but are rarer in the marketing world. A bookalog looks like a book, feels like a book and reads like a book – but it's a lead-generation tool.

The bookalog is one of my key recommendations for investment marketers, especially hedge funds. Though a bookalog is most definitely a marketing vehicle, it is not viewed as a sales piece. It is perceived to be a book, with valuable and useful information to be learned, acted on and passed on to others.

Here's an example of a bookalog I created for one of my clients:

Bookalogs are directly mailed to the investors. Like I do with all elements of a marketing campaign, I recommend testing a bookalog campaign before expanding it. When you see positive results, expand the campaign to reach more investors and to get a greater response.

Most bookalogs are softbound and possess all the aspects of a normal book (i.e. a table of contents, a dedication and an appealing title that makes the recipient want to read it). Most clients want a limited number of hardbound copies as well.

I usually write a 120-page book for my clients.

The bookalog is a positioning instrument for a company and contains valuable information, generally educational in nature.

It shows that the company is an authority on the product or service described within. Creating a definite product differentiation, there is an implication that the product is exceptional enough to be written about in a book.

Bookalogs give a company credibility, and by the time the investor recipient has put down the "book," he or she has learned a great deal. Yet, in reality, the bookalog has one basic and distinct objective, and that is to sell the prospect on generating a lead because they like your company's story.

Michael Gerber wrote and disseminated a "book" titled E-Myth. It became a popular "book," yet in reality it was a publication to sell his consulting services. Over the years, Covenant House has mailed "books" about the Covenant House story of unwed mothers to millions of people nationwide. The book is really a marketing piece to motivate charitable giving and was one of the organization's most successful fundraising activities in its history.

While bookalogs are used by consumers and business-to-business marketers for leads and sales, they are probably the most popular for investment marketers.

Although bookalogs are different from traditional sales pieces, they still follow all the proper direct response copy rules. **Here are six rules you should be aware of as you create your bookalog:**

1. **Copy** needs to follow all of the time-tested direct response copy guidelines (see Chapter 7).

2. **Typeface** should be easy to read and set at 11-point or above.

3. **The bookalog concept** works best when an appropriate personality or authority is involved – I prefer the company president.

4. **A strong order form** at the end of the bookalog should follow all the proper techniques utilized in traditional direct mail pieces, especially the effective use of a Positive Acceptance Statement. This is a key component of increasing response. There is also some evidence that two or three order forms can be valuable, largely due to the "pass along" characteristic of a book.

5. **A simple direct response sales letter in an envelope** should be included with the bookalog. The letter should be no more than one page, providing a reason for reading the book and a rationale of why the individual has received the book.

6. **Testing is crucial** and can be accomplished in a variety of ways. Just like a direct mail letter, results will depend upon the utilization of the right mailing list, superior direct response copy, creative direction of the book and the right offer to generate a lead from the potential investor.

3-D Packages: Powerful
Response Boosters for a Select Group

Marketing to a highly targeted group of investors is a difficult challenge. But one of the most effective ways to get your message to the desired audience with the greatest immediate impact and the highest possible response rate is a three-dimensional package.

3-D marketing uses highly creative oversized or odd-sized packages that have the appearance of a gift. These packages are usually sent via Federal Express or UPS and are designed to get past the mailroom (if mailed to an office) and into the hands of the targeted decision maker.

Even the most jaded investor will find it difficult to resist opening a mysterious package that looks like a gift.

The package might be an odd-sized envelope, a cardboard or wooden box or a tube. The contents could be a jigsaw puzzle with missing pieces, the beginning of a collection of special items, a lock with an offer to deliver the key – or a variety of other items that come from an especially creative imagination.

The results from 3-D mailings are usually very positive. These intrusive hands-on pieces usually trigger a response rate that is five to 50 times the normal rate of a traditional mailing piece.

But this should be considered only to a select subset of highly targeted investors because the price per piece is so high. Our target audience for 3-D packages is usually 500–1,000.

With a 3-D campaign, you're able to break through the clutter, dramatically make your presentation and set the stage for your phone or sales call. If the prospect doesn't call first, a good salesperson will initiate a call with the reminder: "We're the company that sent you the...." It's amazing how creative three-dimensional packages break down barriers.

Videolog: A Marketing Breakthrough that Creates a "WOW" Factor

Videologs make a powerful impact and are ideal for sending to high-end prospects.

A videolog is one of the newest technological advancements in direct response marketing. They are special mail pieces that automatically play a video when opened up by the investor. A screen is included on the piece itself, which is opened up like a brochure.

Videologs demand attention ... and command response.

They are stunning pieces that have probably never been seen by your prospect before.

The video itself can be two minutes, three minutes or 30 minutes. And it can have a large or small screen. It can even have a button to make a phone call to respond to your offer, without ever touching a cell phone.

For the videolog, I create a powerful direct response video with the proper copy. It's delivered in an envelope with a cover letter, a small brochure that has the video and a lift note. The impact is stellar.

When created with direct response rules in mind, the direct mail formats described can deliver powerful response from investors.

Which format is best for you? It really depends on your objectives, company product/service, minimum investment, offer and more.

Your direct mail package will be the core of your lead-generation program, so choosing your format properly will help you to be more successful in attracting new investors.

CHAPTER 11
Email: Effective Communication or Waste of Time?

Email campaigns can be effective, but cannot be used on their own. Resist the urge to rely on email alone.

Email should only be going to the names that you also use for direct mail.

For an integrated campaign, I create a pre-emailing (an email that hits before the direct mail is received) and post-emailing (an email hitting after the direct mail) and emails in between.

In fact, I usually create a series of seven emails to the same prospects.

There are several critical components that need to be considered when creating an effective email strategy for your equity crowdfunding campaign.

The first is the subject line.

Subject Lines: The Opener That Can Make all the Difference

It's critical that you test different subject lines.

The goal of a subject line is to create curiosity about content, to entice your prospect to read further. Even the most experienced direct response marketer can guess wrong.

But the marketplace is never wrong.

35% of email recipients have cited the subject line as the most important factor motivating them to open an email. Not surprising, since the average person weeds through more than 2,200 spam emails every year – and that's after more than 90% of them have already been stopped with filters.

For an investment opportunity in uranium, I sent out 1 million emails with the same content.

The first 500,000 were sent with the subject line: February Subscriber Alert: Uranium. The second 500,000 emails were sent with the subject line: Runaway Uranium Stock Boom.

If you guessed Runaway Uranium Stock Boom was more successful, you were right. The email with this subject line created an 11.55% better response than the first one.

Try using specifics and words that create emotion and curiosity in your subject lines.

Here's another example of subject lines I ran for an investment newsletter:

Subject line #1:

Why 94% of my stock recommendations made money.

Subject line #2:

How my picks made 22.92% when the S&P 500 lost nearly 19%.

Which do you think worked best?

If you picked No. 1, you were right. It got a 10.53% response rate, compared to a 6.8% for No. 2.

Body of the Email

It may seem counterintuitive, but pretty emails with lots of graphics don't get as much response as plain text emails.

In fact, plain text emails yield 17% more clicks than HTML-designed emails.

Both plain text and HTML have the same open rates, but when a reader is focused on a single-link text based email instead of a more visually stimulating HTML email, he or she is more likely to click on the call-to-action (CTA).

Here is an example of an email I created for my client StarShop, shown at the right.

New Mobile App Could Disrupt a Rapidly Growing $5.4 Billion Industry and Give Investors a Ground Floor Private—Not Public—Investment Opportunity

Dear _____,

My name is Kevin Harrington. You may know me as one of the original "sharks" on the ABC TV show *Shark Tank*.

As you may know, the investment opportunities I've evaluated on *Shark Tank* have been reserved primarily for "sharks."

But now that's all changed. I've created an opportunity where **you can invest** in a company geared to **quickly disrupt a rapidly growing industry**.

The company is **StarShop** – and they've put together a dynamic mobile shopping app that uses celebrities and videos to sell products.

Thanks to a highly potent combination of celebrity influence, social media and mobile shopping, **StarShop** is right now **poised to take full advantage of the massive, unstoppable trend in mobile app growth.**

A full report about this unique investment opportunity has been mailed to your postal mailbox and should arrive at any time. Click here for an online version.

With an aggressive growth plan, this investment could deliver strong profit potential to those investors who get in on the ground floor.

The recent explosion in value for mobile apps – with app-makers selling in 2016 for as much as $5.9 billion! – means that StarShop comes along at the perfect time to take advantage of this huge upward trend.

Investing in **StarShop** gives you the chance to join me in an investment where my partners and I are looking for explosive growth.

This is YOUR opportunity to invest with the "sharks."

Call 1-866-506-2720 today to speak with a representative about this exclusive private investment – and to claim your free investor's kit.

This kit includes three free in-depth research reports that explain in clear detail how this opportunity works…and how you can get in on the ground floor.

You'll also discover how becoming a StarShop investor will entitle you to "VIP Access" to a number of our exclusive StarShop celebrity events over the next 12 months.

Your email should also be easy to scan and present the most important information at the top.

It should match your offer and your direct mail package and present a clear call-to-action (CTA).

Here are seven key rules for email I've developed as applied to your equity crowdfunding campaign:

1. **Emails are going to be the most effective** when they are sent to the same names on the postal direct mail list of investors.

2. **Emails have the greatest impact** after investors have already received your direct mail package. When prospects receive a follow-up email, it reinforces your offer and generates a greater response.

3. **Even a higher response occurs** when emails come before and after the direct mail piece hits the prospect's mailbox. For example, the investor will receive an email telling them that they should expect to receive something soon in the mail. Then another email arrives to follow up the direct mail package.

4. **The email should never be a sales message only** – it will depress your response. It needs to be informational with perceived value. It should be a value-added informational letter. Your prospect learns something and sees that it's in his or her self-interest to read. High-pressure sales copy will kill email response and your relationship to the prospect. Informational value-added emails create relationships and response.

5. **The email should only use direct response copy.** It should never use traditional advertorial copy that depresses response. To review the principles of direct response copy, go to Chapter 7.

6. **Email can be highly effective** when it includes a valuable informational video. The video increases your

open rates and click-through rates. I'll cover more on how to create powerful video content in Chapter 18.

7. **The email has to promote your offer/premium**, not the investment itself.

These are just some of the key rules that I follow based upon our 30 years of experience with over 100 million emails we have sent out for clients, and literally hundreds of tests we have used to verify what produces the highest return.

You should not rely on email alone because your cost per lead and cost per sale will be higher. And, there are often more names available on postal lists than on email lists. For example, if you are marketing under Reg 506C, the email universe for the accredited investor is 3,020,093 names. That's less than for direct mail.

In Chapter 21, you'll also read about email strategy for a conversion series.

By sending a regular email newsletter, you can help position what you're doing, increase your credibility and remind your prospects of your offer. Email newsletters can help build a relationship with the investor, which is critical to your integrated campaign.

Finally, your online campaign should include retargeting, which I'll cover in Chapter 15.

When you follow the rules and principles I've outlined above, email marketing can be a powerful component of your equity crowdfunding campaign. Email helps to increase response and reinforce your message, so that you can get the attention and the sign-on of investors who will partner with you in your business or venture.

CHAPTER 12
Banner Ads: An Essential Key to Lead Generation

Banner ads run on Google, Bing and other platforms. They deliver a small amount of information, grab the attention of a prospect and drive them to your landing page.

I use banner ads in two ways.

First, I target the ads just to the names from a custom list.

Second, I target them to a look-a-like audience.

Here is an example of a banner ad aimed at investors. Prospects would see this ad after they've already received the direct mail piece.

Online banner ads can be used to effectively remarket your investment opportunity to a tight universe of investor prospects.

Investor Spotlight:

"$15 Trillion Market Disruption Underway"

Little-known company's disruptive technology has triggered explosive growth setting up an unprecedented opportunity for investors.

New "Mini-IPO" opens the door for YOU to get in on the ground floor.

Full report here.

And they can also be used to expand your prospect base by driving new prospects to your page.

Banner ads are powerful tools that cannot be overlooked in your campaign.

In creating and testing banner ads, I have found several tactics that will increase response.

Here are six powerful lead generation tactics for using banner ads effectively in your equity crowdfunding campaign.

Tactic #1: Editorial Banner Ads

A winning format for all banner ads are "editorial" ads.

Editorial ads produce better response than non-editorial ads or ads that look too sales-y. The example ad on page 81 is a unique investment opportunity for one of my clients.

This type of banner ad delivers an insight or piece of information that will cause the investor to become intrigued or interested in reading further.

Tactic #2: Different Headlines

70% of the success or failure of your ad is the headline.

It might seem counterintuitive, but longer headlines generate a higher response than shorter headlines.

More words and more characters done right mean more click-throughs for your online ads.

In fact, headlines between 90 and 99 characters received a click-through rate that was 0.43% higher than headlines that had less than 90 characters.

Headlines with more words also gained a higher response. Take a look at the headline below, created for an investment client:

New "Mini IPO" Toolkit:
The new SEC law creates a ground floor opportunity for investors.
Under the Jobs Act, investors can now invest in a "Mini-IPO" before the company becomes public. This gives Investors the potential of "insider" type profits for the first time. All the details are available in this free toolkit. Click here.

These reports are free. click here for details.

In another test, headlines with just 16 words achieved a click-through rate of 0.33%, while short headlines of just four words got a click-through rate of 0.14%.

Take a look at the following test:

Headline #1:

"If you're hungry for 500% profits, this internationally

known pizza brand is ready to deliver."

Headline #2:

"Fast food, fast profits"

Headline #1 got a higher response, with more detailed, specific copy, more words and more characters.

Tactic #3: Video vs. Report

Banner ads that offer a video will get a better response than banner ads that don't.

However, advertising a free online report along with the video will help you get an even higher response rate.

Tactic #4: Matching Landing Pages

For banner ads to be effective, they must link to landing pages that match the headlines and content of the ad.

I recently tested six different banner ads, each with its own headline. And each one had a landing page that matched the headline of the ad. Banner ads that linked to "matching" landing pages received a higher response than the ads that linked to one general landing page.

Tactic #5: Media Strategy

Banner ads are only as good as where you place them. You must make sure you are placing them appropriately. Test! Don't rely on Google or a service to do this for you. Evaluate each media placement for effectiveness.

Tactic #6: Test, Test, Test

Test your headlines, ad placement and graphics to see which banner ads perform the best.

Remember that testing is the backbone of direct response marketing. When you are able to assess results, you'll be able to refine and rework your campaign to increase response rate.

That's why I test everything that can affect response. You always want to test. Test to find what is more effective and what will increase response. You need to test the media. You need to test the size of the ad. You need to test copy. Always test (Learn more about testing in Chapter 20).

Take a look at the test on the right-hand page:

- The ad on the left got a click-through rate of 0.07%, which means that out of every 1,000 impressions, seven people clicked on the ad.

- The ad on the right got a click-through rate of 0.13%, which means that out of every 1,000 impressions, 13 people clicked on the ad.

In terms of performance (measured by click-through rate), the ad with a longer headline outperformed the ad with the shorter headline by almost 2 to 1.

Banner ads will be a critical part of your campaign in marketing to the investor. They not only expand your prospect base, but they are an essential tool in retargeting, which I'll cover in greater detail in Chapter 15.

CHAPTER 13

Facebook: 8 Critical Tools for Your Equity Crowdfunding Campaign

Facebook is one of the equity crowdfunding marketers' best friends.

Right now, I often use at least 20% of a marketing budget on Facebook.

This medium is accountable. It's great to test. And it dramatically expands your universe of prospects...allowing you to raise more funds. One of the best things about Facebook is that it keeps expanding its services and effectiveness, so that you can get a better return on your efforts.

And it's great for those who are marketing under Reg A+ or under Reg 506C.

But Facebook must be used correctly. You need to do more than create ads or posts to generate interest. When you know how to harness this powerful tool, you'll see massive response and build your prospect base.

Here are eight tools for using Facebook for equity crowdfunding marketing:

Tool #1: An Integrated, Multichannel Approach

Advertise on Facebook to the same people who are

receiving your direct mail and email, and seeing your pre-roll commercials and banner ads.

Prospects who would have seen the ad on page 87, created for my client Starshop, would have also received their magalog and emails and seen their additional digital ads.

This type of integrated strategy increases your response from your Facebook efforts. Additionally, it raises response rates for your email, pre-roll commercials, banner ads and other marketing materials.

Tool #2: Facebook Custom Lists

This powerful tactic allows you to identify the Facebook accounts of prospects on your profiled investor list. This way, you can retarget investors who have received your mail.

You can segment your Facebook custom list any way you want. Then a marketing campaign to the targeted customer is initiated only on your supplied list. In this way, you market to targeted customers on their newsfeeds. Using a custom list, I was able to display the ad for Starshop on the previous page in the newsfeeds of their prospects.

A Facebook custom list can be extremely powerful, as shown by the following example:

Volvo's Construction Equipment division (Volvo CE) targeted American and Canadian prospects who were already connected with Volvo competitors.

The company also targeted prospects similar to their current customers, age 23 and older.

The Volvo CE Facebook ad generated 300,000 impressions; 9,485 clicks; and finally, 27 qualified leads!

With $2,000 coming in with every lead, Volvo CE enjoyed a 30% cost reduction.

Tool #3: Look-a-like Audiences

Look-a-like audiences are audiences that look and behave like your best prospects. They can be created in a variety of ways, all of which I will cover in Chapter 16.

For Facebook look-a-like audiences, I have discovered little-known ways to make the look-a-like feature of Facebook perform better than the strategies of most digital "experts."

You start with a direct mail transactional model list, create a custom list and then use it to create a Facebook look-a-like audience. It's a look-a-like audience on steroids.

Remember, a look-a-like audience is where Facebook algorithms review data and habits to identify prospects that look just like your current leads.

Using Facebook, marketers are now reaching prospects they never thought they could communicate with before.

Above, see a Facebook ad that I created for look-a-like audiences for Real Water.

Tool #4: Retargeting for Increased Response

Retargeting is an awesome way to increase your profitability with Facebook. Your Facebook ad will follow your investor prospects wherever they go, and draws your prospects back to your website and your offer.

I'll cover retargeting in greater detail in Chapter 15.

Tool #5: Newsfeed vs Display/Right Side Ads

Concentrate your efforts on newsfeed ads, rather than advertising on the right-hand side. Ads that are shown directly on the center of the page get better results.

Tool #6: Seven Lines of Sizzling
Direct Response Teaser Copy

Facebook limits the amount of copy that will be immediately visible to a viewer. That means you have seven lines to draw in the prospect with direct response copy and persuade them to follow your call-to-action (CTA).

Select hot words such as "new," "now," "easy," "introducing" and "save." Teaser copy should create interest and curiosity, and get your prospect to take action.

Remember, this applies to your headline too.

Tool #7: Powerful Video

Video generates powerful response and engagement on Facebook. Video creates curiosity and, if done well, it can powerfully communicate your offer and investment opportunity.

But your video must follow specific principles. If you use powerful direct response video on Facebook, you will get more leads and shareholders.

Here are four "musts" for a successful Facebook video campaign:

1. Have powerful teaser text at the start to drive a click.

2. Use text during the video. Facebook will favor your ad, and viewers like it. You'll get better response.

3. Have a powerful call-to-action (CTA) at the end to drive viewers to your landing page. "Watch more," "Download

now" and "Join now for a special discount" get more action.

4. Make sure the video follows the direct response rules for copy, art and offer.

I'll cover more on video strategy in Chapter 18.

Tool #8: Facebook Leads

Facebook leads allow you to collect contact information of investors, expanding your prospect base.

I recommend that you create a specific campaign for lead generation so that you can automatically collect contact information for follow-up. When a prospect expresses interest, Facebook will automatically fill out the inquiry form for you.

Remember, Facebook by itself will not provide you with the investors you need. But by combining Facebook ads with other media, you'll generate quality shareholders with this cost-effective medium.

You'll be able to retarget prospects you may have otherwise lost, increase response and generate new leads for your equity crowdfunding campaign...getting you closer to your goal of fundraising X amount for your business or venture.

CHAPTER 14
Pre-Roll Profits: The Commercial Before the Video

Video can be placed and utilized on a variety of platforms that will speak to the investor in a unique and powerful way.

In fact, video keeps getting better and more targeted.

One of the most powerful video placements is an advertisement on YouTube that you can target to your prospects.

This is how it works: If you've ever watched a video on YouTube, you've probably had to wait anywhere from a few seconds to a couple minutes to watch the video you clicked on.

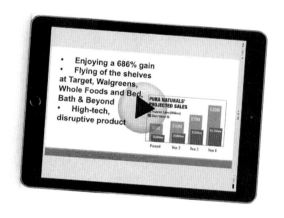

First, you were shown a video ad or commercial. This is called a pre-roll video and it's one of the growing techniques used to target a specific audience. Pre-roll videos are a powerful strategy for targeting investors with your investment opportunity.

Google TrueView places the advertising spots in the pre-roll before a YouTube video. Using a growing set of variables, you can accurately target the investors you're looking for.

Here's how I am currently using pre-roll videos for an equity crowdfunding campaign:

- I am only doing pre-rolls on select investor cable channels that match our psychographic.
- I am also using our pre-selected email/postal list to run the ads only to our target audience when they watch a video on YouTube.
- I am using a look-a-like audience of investors to target the pre-roll video, based on the investor prospect list provided.

With one investor campaign I executed, I attracted 36,589 pre-roll views.

Here are seven things you need to know about pre-roll videos:

1: **They work.** Pre-roll commercials have an average click-through rate of 1.84%, higher than any other type of digital ad. In fact, the average online video viewer spends 16 minutes a month watching video ads.

2: **The first three seconds of your video are the most important,** especially for pre-roll videos. If you lose the attention of viewers, they are going to click "skip ad" if given the option. Immediately catch the interest of the investor or your opportunity to gain a new lead or prospect will be lost.

3: **The call-to-action (CTA) is the second most important element** in your pre-roll video. The investor should be able to respond immediately.

4: **Pre-rolls can be specifically targeted to your audience.** Want investors? Done. Want alternative health customers? Done. Want conservatives? Done.

5: **Pre-roll gives you the advantage of better Search Engine Optimization (SEO)**…on YouTube and Google.

6: **Pre-roll videos can have multiple uses** … on your landing page, in banner/Facebook ads and in emails.

7: YouTube is now providing special buttons for pre-roll videos that say, "Shop Now", which can easily be converted to "Subscribe Now", "Donate Now", "attend this event", etc.

Pre-roll videos are one of the most powerful, effective components of your equity crowdfunding campaign. A pre-roll video can increase response from current prospects, and expand leads when used with look-a-like audiences.

To learn more about how to create powerful video you can use for pre-roll commercials, go to Chapter 18.

CHAPTER 15
Retargeting to Dramatically Boost Response

By now, you've learned the importance of creating an integrated and multichannel marketing campaign.

What happens when your marketing materials get a response…prospects visit your landing page…and then leave, without responding to your offer?

A key component of your integrated campaign will be to retarget prospects who have already responded to your ads and visited your landing page.

Retargeting gives you greater return on your marketing efforts and massively increases lead generation.

In this chapter, I'll dive deeper into the details of retargeting ads described in previous chapters.

When used by themselves, Facebook ads, banner ads and pre-roll ads can be effective. But when combined with retargeting, they can dramatically increase your number of leads and new investors – and lower your overall marketing cost per lead and cost per sale.

Retargeting allows you to remind prospects of your powerful offer and entice them to return to the landing page and invest in your business.

The best response to any banner ad or Facebook campaign comes from retargeting.

By retargeting investors, you're reaching close to 100% of your best audience prospects in a powerful way.

So, how is retargeting done?

Here's how I do it for equity crowdfunding campaigns:

I create banner or Facebook ads specifically for those investors who have already visited your landing page. The ad is compatible with the direct mail, email or other media message used in the campaign.

When prospects come to your landing page – whether through direct mail, email or other media – I put retargeting codes on their devices so that your specific retargeting ad will follow them around the internet.

To make retargeting work well, the ad needs to use powerful direct response copy. As explained in Chapter 12 on banner ads, I usually create an editorial looking ad to generate a higher response.

Your offer and/or call-to-action (CTA) are critical. For example, you may want to show a video and offer a free special report. But it's easy to test to see what kind of offer will work for you.

Here are some retargeting ads I've created that have proven to successfully remarket investment opportunities.

Investment Spotlight:
High-Tech Health Breakthrough Offers Explosive Profit Potential

One little-known company's proprietary technology has produced a game-changing natural health product that is right now flying off the shelves at Whole Foods, Costco and other supermarkets.

Investors now have the chance to get in before shares trade on any public exchange ... with possible gains of up to 300%.

Free report available here.

FinTech Investing:
Mobile Banking Revolution Triggers Historic Invest Opportunity

#1-Rated Tech Investor Rick Currin's New Top Pick
• Available in 164 countries
• Numerous key partnerships
• Creating massive disruption in the banking industry
• Mobile app breakthrough

Investors are now rushing to cash in on the global paradigm shift away from "big banks" and into mobile payments.

Brick-and-mortar banks are about to go the way of the payphone — and one little-known company provides investors with the single best way to cash in on this unstoppable megatrend.

See what #1-rated tech expert Rick Currin says about the technology ...

Full video briefing here.

Retargeting is a game changer.

It can dramatically increase your response, help you gain more leads, reinforce your marketing campaign and increase your profits.

It's an essential strategy in your equity crowdfunding campaign.

CHAPTER 16
How to Supercharge Your Marketing with Look-a-like Audiences

With a targeted investor audience, you'll be able to get a high response and generate new leads.

What if I told you that there was a way to reach investors just like your best prospects?

They behave the same, are interested in the same things and share very similar demographics.

A look-a-like audience, like retargeting, will be one of your most valuable tools in your integrated and multichannel campaign to the investor.

If done right, look-a-like audiences can dramatically expand your prospects, grow leads and increase the number of new customers like never before.

There are multiple ways to build a look-a-like audience on different platforms.

In this chapter, I'll explain how to create look-a-like audiences on the following eight platforms in greater detail:
- Transactional Data
- Facebook
- Google
- AdRoll Prospecting
- Bing
- Pre-Roll
- Amazon
- Private companies

Let's look at how each of these differ … and how you can supercharge your look-a-like quality and response with a little-known strategy I developed for my clients.

Platform #1: Look-a-like Audiences
Built with Transactional Data

Transactional data is generated from purchases. It has detailed information about the buying habits and demographics of prospects. Using this valuable information, you'll be able to create highly strategic audiences that are virtual clones of your own current customers.

It's so advanced that today I can create a look-a-like audience that matches 90-95% of the original audience's qualities.

These kinds of look-a-like audiences use transactional data generated from thousands of customers to find your right prospect. This is the best look-a-like tactic, because it's based on purchases, not searches, likes or viewing habits.

For example, transactional data includes extensive and powerful data on every kind of purchase – for example, of stocks, nutritional supplements, clothing, wine or any other kind of product or service. It then generates direct mail names (and in other cases, email) for you to use to expand your strategic audience.

Large database management companies like Oracle store thousands of data tags on prospects. For my clients, I work with behavioral scientists and engineers to match them to a precise product or service profile, then create the look-a-like audience. It enables us to get a much higher response, doubling it over traditional efforts in some cases.

Data modeling – if done right – is revolutionary. It will supercharge your response … and dramatically increase your universe of profitable prospect names of investors who are likely to respond to your offer.

Using transactional data to build look-a-like audiences works especially well if you have a customer list of 5,000 or more names. In this case, the "closing" is miraculous.

LOOK-A-LIKE AUDIENCE

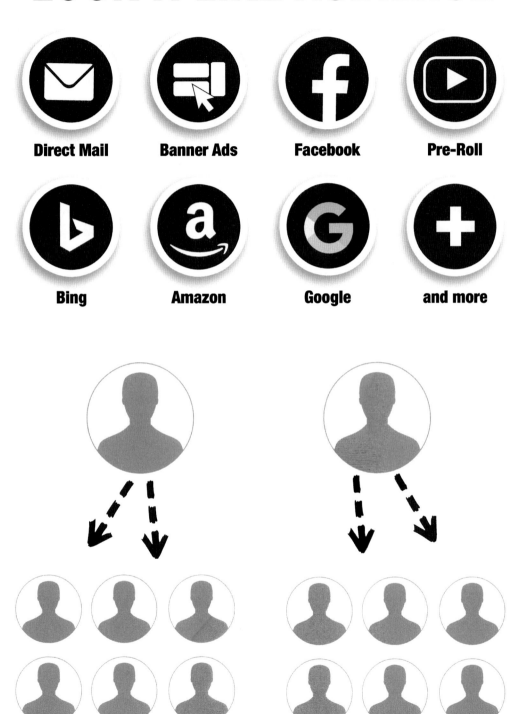

Direct Mail   Banner Ads   Facebook   Pre-Roll

Bing   Amazon   Google   and more

Platform#2 Facebook Look-a-like Audiences

As I discussed in Chapter 13, another great way to build a look-a-like audience is by tapping into Facebook's algorithms.

Facebook keeps perfecting its ability to duplicate clones of your customers. And while the results aren't as good as transactional data, they come pretty close.

Using these algorithms, I can identify the common qualities of your prospects and find similar audiences on Facebook.

Facebook locates new prospects based on similar profiles and online behavior. What do they click on? What do they like or comment on? Facebook will create a look-a-like audience that matches the behavior and the characteristics of the prospects you have identified. This includes analyzing data such as page likes, demographics, interests, website visits and more.

Our very best results occur when I take a model built on transactional data of a customer file and use it as a source audience to create a look-a-like audience on Facebook.

You can choose the size of a look-a-like audience during the creation process.

A smaller look-a-like audience will more closely match your source audience.

Larger look-a-like audiences increase your potential reach, but they reduce the level of similarity between look-a-like and source audiences.

However, the larger your customer list or source audience, the more accurate your look-a-like audience will be.

A source audience of between 4,000 and 50,000 works best.

And if your source audience is made up of your best customers rather than all of your customers, that could lead to improved results.

Platform #3 Google Similar Audiences

Google uses data collected in the Google Display Network to prospect. Data includes demographics, searches, video views, website visits, application downloads and more. They use a type of artificial intelligence to analyze trillions of searches and activity across millions of websites to help figure out when people are close to buying.

Again, using transactional data and/or your customer files with this approach will dramatically improve results.

Platform #4 AdRoll Prospecting
Look-a-like Audiences

AdRoll finds audiences using the IntentMap, the largest proprietary data co-op that advertisers can access by contributing their site data.

About 5,000 advertisers of all sizes have opted into IntentMap, pooling more than 1.2 billion digital profiles from across the web and mobile sources.

Such diversity allows AdRoll Prospecting to perform for all verticals and find you prospects.

If you want to make this work even better, use transactional data and/or customer data.

Platform #5 Bing Look-a-like Audiences

Bing Ads now has a look-a-like feature.

Bing's in-market audiences allow marketers to target consumers who appear to be on the verge of making purchases. Grabbing someone's attention when they're ready to purchase is a powerful strategy.

Bing's in-market audiences focus on 14 different targets: four are dedicated to finance, three to travel, two to cars.

Others include clothing, hobbies, leisure, toys and games.

And more in-market audience targets are on the way.

Platform #6 Pre-Roll Look-a-like Audiences

Having created more than 400 TV commercials and videos, I love integrating video into a campaign. Pre-rolls are a big breakthrough.

You can create a look-a-like audience for your pre-roll video on YouTube, using transactional data and/or customer list. This is a powerful strategy to ensure similar audiences see your video ad.

Platform #7 Amazon Look-a-like Audiences

One of the most targeted and effective ways to build a look-a-like audience is on Amazon, which I'll cover more in Chapter 17.

Look-a-like audiences on Amazon rely on transactional data, which creates the most accurate look-a-like audience possible.

Platform #8 Private Companies Look-a-like Audiences

Many other private companies are using different ways to create look-a-like audiences.

For example, I'm successfully using a database actually built on credit data.

And another I'm testing now integrates transactional data and web searches using transactional data based on a co-op of websites.

Look-a-like audiences are an extremely effective way to expand reach and target prospects who will respond to your investment opportunity.

Should you use just one platform for look-a-like audiences? No!

I use all eight and my clients love the results.

For each company and each of the systems, I use slightly different models.

The results of using a look-a-like audience include:

- Better Return on Investment (ROI)
- Greater enlargement of your prospect universe
- Higher profits

For these reasons, I use all look-a-like audiences. I have one campaign now that's divided 40/20/10 with different look-a-like audiences.

One of the keys to success beyond proper testing is knowing how to create the models yourself.

I've learned you should never rely on the modeling company. They are statisticians.

They are not marketers who understand the peculiarities of each target market.

That's why I have trained my staff to modify and adjust each model based on solid direct response psychographic market principles, knowledge and experience.

Building look-a-like audiences will significantly elevate your marketing efforts by creating responsive new leads and by powerfully expanding your investor prospect base.

CHAPTER 17
The Surprising Power of Amazon-Generated Data to Reach Investors

You might be surprised to learn that Amazon may be one of your most powerful tools for reaching investors.

Amazon is not just a retailer...it holds a massive database of information about the purchasing habits of consumers. This information can give you the insights you need to target prospects on Amazon's site by serving them highly targeted ads.

Here are four ways to expand your reach on Amazon:

1. Target and retarget using a "pixel."

The first step to effectively targeting – and retargeting – prospects on Amazon with ads is to use a special pixel on your own homepage. This pixel allows you to identify those customers who are visiting your own homepage and shopping on Amazon...so that you can see where "audience overlap" occurs on both sites.

So, when your leads go to Amazon, they see your offer in targeted ads.

2. Use a custom list to expand reach.

One of the most powerful ways to target investors on Amazon is to upload your existing customer or prospect file to the site. Using your own custom list will allow you to serve ads to a highly targeted audience.

3. Build look-a-like audiences.

You can also build a look-a-like audience on Amazon using

information from the pixel on your own site to expand your reach and increase conversion.

Amazon uses their own transactional data to reach new prospects that look and behave just like your best customers and prospects.

What makes this even better than Google or Facebook and other similar platforms is that it doesn't rely on algorithms. Look-a-like audiences on Amazon use transactional data, creating a highly specific and targeted audience.

4. Target prospects using lifestyle, in-market and demographics.

Lifestyle

Amazon will provide you with powerful data that allows you to examine the search patterns, browsing habits and purchase behaviors of prospects to serve them targeted ads.

For example, you can target and identify segments of prospects based on their general lifestyle interests.

In-Market

In-market targeting segments allow you to identify and reach customers who have searched for a product in a specific category over the past 30 days.

Demographics

Amazon will also allow you to target audience segments based on demographics. For example, you can target leads based on gender, age, income and even number of children.

When used with these strategies, Amazon can become one of your most effective and targeted methods for reaching investors with your equity crowdfunding campaign.

CHAPTER 18
Video: The Power You Should Not Ignore

Video brings your product or service to life in ways that print cannot, with demonstrations, testimonials and benefits in action. It's a powerful way to deliver your message to prospects – and generate leads and sales.

I love video. In fact, I started my career in infomercials, and I've created over 400 videos and TV commercials (including 13 infomercials). I have seen the effectiveness and power of this media, again and again.

Video can be used on your landing page (in fact, it should be used on your landing page); on Facebook ads; in banner ads; in videologs; and more.

Video does not need to be complicated. It can be formatted simply, with mostly words on a plain background, interspersed sparingly with appropriate graphic images. A strong voice-over reads the script with passion and excitement, creating a powerful response.

Even if the investor does not watch the entire video on your landing page, video increases your credibility, which ultimately boosts leads and sales.

Often, an investment decision requires that more than one person "say yes" to the opportunity. A video allows the investor's spouse, friend or other family member to engage in the decision-making process, helping prospects to overcome fear, objections and the difficulty of explaining the

opportunity to someone else.

Video for marketing to the investor has four key purposes:

1. Video is a powerful, compelling tease that can be used in your banner ad, email and Facebook marketing. Using video on Facebook not only increases response, but also increases reach. In fact, Facebook favors video...and they prefer text on the video.

2. Video provides credibility when used on the landing page, even if visitors don't view it or only watch a portion of it.

3. Video helps increase response from the investor, especially on the landing page.

4. Video is a useful tool in your conversion process, including part of the conversion series or due diligence process.

The bottom line is that a direct response video should be part of your campaign to the investor. It's a powerful way to increase response and enhance your credibility.

Here are 19 critical rules for video that will help you produce outstanding results and get the response you're looking for.

Rule #1: The first few seconds of your video are key. You've got to capture the attention of the investor immediately. It's easy to skip a video, so make sure the first few seconds are powerful, and deliver your message clearly.

Don't start with a fade-in from a black screen – instead, use vibrant, colorful images to immediately engage the viewer.

Rule #2: Use only direct response copy in your script. Your script should have one clear theme. It must be benefit-oriented and guide your viewer through the principles of AIDA: It should draw attention, attract interest, develop desire and compel action.

Remember, the video needs to use direct response copy to produce a high response. This is not the time to use journalistic or traditional advertising copy. That would kill the sale. Your video is a story designed to get people to buy your product or service, or generate that lead.

Rule #3: Use a credible spokesperson to demonstrate benefits. Seeing the benefits in action – and hearing the opportunity discussed by the spokesperson – are powerful.

A spokesperson can be more effective than sheer entertainment … but that doesn't mean your video can't be fun. For example, I cast a 4-year old as "the world's greatest investment trader" in a client's online video. It was entertaining, informative and effective.

Rule #4: Repeat your unique selling proposition (USP). Just as you should feature your USP at the beginning, in the middle and at the end of every print campaign, you also need it in your video. Be sure it's consistent with the rest of your branding and collateral materials.

Rule #5: PowerPoint v. action. The video style that is the most effective for a target audience of investors is a video with PowerPoint words, or something called a "storybook" video. Using text with video increases retention and response.

Rule #6: Use text. Whether you're using a live personality or a PowerPoint, you can use on-screen text to lengthen the time that a prospect will watch a video – and how likely they are to respond to your offer. Make sure that the words properly reflect what's being said, are easy to read and stay in one location.

Facebook actually says that using printed words increases video engagement by an average of 12%. If you're not sure how to add text to your video, Facebook has a tool that makes it easy to add word captions to your videos.

Rule #7: Use testimonials and/or reviews with ratings. Testimonials are one of the most powerful sales tools in existence. But remember, investors want to see real people who like your product.

Showing a person who is not a professional actor or model – someone who seems uncomfortable and whose story is not overly rehearsed – actually increases your response.

When you're filming customer testimonials, shoot them several times so you can edit exactly what you want from the answers. IPhone testimonials are great, too!

Rule #8: Connect the script with the prospect quickly and dramatically. Like the copy you use for direct mail, email and other marketing materials, a powerful direct response script will hit hard immediately.

Drama. Suspense. Surprise. No warm-up. No introduction. Command attention.

Remember…47% of the value of a video is delivered within the first three seconds, and 74% in the first ten.

Rule #9: Length – fear not. Do not be afraid of a longer video. Some of the most powerful videos are 12 minutes long. When considering video length, ask yourself the following questions: How complicated are your benefits to explain? How easy is it to overcome objections?

For marketing to investors, I normally create three- to 12-minute videos.

Rule #10: Get a model release. Always get a model release from those you're filming so you have the right to use your footage wherever you want to, whether that be on your landing page, Facebook, banner ads or elsewhere. You may also want to use footage in creative ways, for example using a still photo and an excerpt from the testimonial in a brochure.

Rule #11: Have a strong call-to-action (CTA). Your job is to make it as easy as possible for the viewer to respond … whether you show a phone number, email address, URL or mailing address.

Rule #12: Graphics add power. The addition of graphics in the right places will increase viewer retention and reinforce your message. Every image must reflect the value of your investment opportunity.

Rule #13: Optimize your video for silent mode. Believe it or not, 85% of people watch Facebook videos on silent. That means that you'll have to create drama and impact without relying on a voiceover or background music.

Instead, communicate your message with powerful action and show important words as text on screen.

Rule #14: Clean and simple win on small screens. Remember that many of your prospects will be watching your video on mobile screens. Avoid small text and detailed visuals, and keep your graphics simple and bold. This is a key detail when choosing your thumbnail image, which should be clean and bright to catch the eye of your viewers.

Your title doesn't need to be included in the thumbnail – you can attach metadata to the file when you share it online.

Rule #15: The camera is unforgiving. Consider how the subjects you're filming appear through the lens. Don't neglect wardrobe considerations. An outrageously patterned tie or an electric blue dress can distract viewers from the content.

Take extra time to see what doesn't belong in the shot. For example, a newspaper or magazine showing a headline can immediately date your production and limit its use.

Rule #16: Remember Murphy's Law. If something can go wrong, it will.

Plan, plan, plan! If you don't bring it to your video shoot, you're sure to need it. If you don't have a Plan B, you'll need one. Outline everything you'll need, including rolls and rolls of duct tape, and take special care with cameras and other equipment that may become victims of carelessness.

Look into getting insurance for the day of the shoot that includes weather, equipment and both personal and corporate liability.

Rule #17: Allow for extra shots. Always shoot more footage than you need, since you'll always need more than you thought. Even if you think a scene is "perfect," shoot a backup so you can pick from the best material as you edit.

Make time for "establishing shots" – shots that show the context of what's being sold. Shoot "reaction shots" to show one person reacting to another's comments. This is called "B-roll" footage, which can be invaluable during editing.

Rule #18: Maximize its use. Brainstorm multiple uses for your video – as a premium, as a download or to drive investors to your URL.

Rule #19: Enlist the right crew. Remember, it was direct response marketers who perfected the infomercial. And the infomercial is still highly effective today.

It's important to use direct response marketing professionals, not video professionals or general ad agencies, to get the most out of your video.

Video will be an essential component of your marketing campaign to the investor. It's a powerful way to communicate your offer, increase response, gain credibility and win investors.

By following these 19 rules, you'll develop an effective video that you can use on your landing page, Facebook ads, email marketing and more.

CHAPTER 19
The Key Question: Your Spokesperson

As you have seen, I've outlined all the critical components of your integrated marketing campaign to the investor: your landing page, direct mail, email marketing, banner ads, Facebook ads, retargeting, look-a-like audiences, video and pre-roll commercials.

Maybe you've been brainstorming what these elements will look like in your equity crowdfunding marketing campaign.

Maybe you've been thinking about your unique selling proposition (USP), how you will communicate your offer with direct response copy, what kind of video you will create…but have you thought of your spokesperson?

Your spokesperson is one of your critical keys to success that will help you generate leads and get investors to respond to your offer.

Your spokesperson is your "voice" for generating the investor lead – and your voice in the conversion process.

Consider the following questions:

- Who will sign the direct mail letter or email?
- Whose picture will you place on the landing page?
- Who will be the voice of the company?
- Who will be your spokesperson?

These choices can significantly impact response to your campaign, and even make the difference between a campaign that generates massive revenue and one that fails to raise capital.

For an equity crowdfunding campaign, I generally recommend using the company president as the spokesperson.

That being said, there are exceptions to the rule. An

alternative spokesperson can be just as effective. Check out the following examples:

- For one equity crowdfunding client, I used a "Shark Tank" spokesperson.
- Your spokesperson could also be a CPA (Certified Public Accountant).
- Your spokesperson can also be someone with credibility as a financial writer. Often, I'll have an equity crowdfunding campaign where I use an investment newsletter writer.

I do not recommend celebrities, however. They are seldom worth the price. I do not recommend your vice president of marketing or sales. The title alone will depress response.

I have relationships with dozens of quality investment newsletter writers and can help set you up with the right newsletter writer to be your spokesperson.

Your spokesperson is critical to your equity crowdfunding campaign. Consider this choice carefully as you develop your content and your approach.

In the next chapter, I'll cover one of the keystones to direct response marketing: testing.

CHAPTER 20
Testing to Maximize Results

Imagine that you've developed and deployed your crowdfunding campaign – including a landing page, direct mail package, email, Facebook and banner ads, video and retargeting strategy.

But you're not finished yet...

Now comes one of the most decisive parts of your campaign: Testing. Testing can make the difference between marketing efforts that disappoint and marketing efforts that produce outstanding, profit-boosting results.

Testing is the cornerstone of any direct response marketing campaign. Every component of direct marketing media must be accountable.

That's why I call direct response marketing "Accountable Advertising" or "Scientific Advertising."

Testing reduces your risk, gives you valuable marketing intelligence for the future and allows you to constantly increase your response rate.

By testing, you'll learn the following key details:

- You will always know when you spend a dollar and when you get back a dollar...or 75¢ or $1.50.
- You always know your cost per lead.
- You always know your cost per sale.

With any kind of media – direct mail, Facebook, banner ads, email – you'll always know the cost and return on the investment.

You're going to want to test every element of your integrated and multichannel campaign to the investor, using A/B tests to determine the kind of copy, imagery and other variables that get the most response.

You can test headlines, components, email subject lines, different landing pages, banner ads, different email lists… hundreds of variables.

When I put together a campaign, I always choose carefully what to test.

Here is an example of an envelope test I performed for a direct mail campaign. This test consisted of about 60,000 pieces.

In this test, I tested two essential response boosters of the campaign:

1. The postal lists I used

2. The envelope copy, or teaser copy, for which I created two versions: Version A and Version B

I sent two versions of teaser copy to nine different lists.

✓ 100,000-piece mailing, nine different lists

✓ Universe of potential names: 2,965,422

Here are the results of the test:

Cell	Teaser Version A response rate %	Teaser Version B response rate %
List 1	.61	.69
List 2	.40	.34
List 3	.60	.73
List 4	.55	.60
List 5	.36	.46
List 6	.42	.55
List 7	.71	.79
List 8	.65	.72
List 9	.69	.78

As you can see, Version B produced more returns…and became the "control."

With this test, I identified which were the best-performing mailing lists and which version of teaser copy worked best.

Let's say that first, you required a .55 to justify your campaign, and then you only use those list cells performing above a .60.

Second, you can see that Version B significantly outperformed Version A. So, you'll mail Version B and forget about Version A.

Based on what you learn, you'll create a new Version "C" to beat Version "B."

And, you'll test new cells based on the type of investor I have found to be the most responsive – improving results for the next mailing.

Testing is critical to refining your strategy and gaining valuable leads. Don't skip this critical step. It could make a massive difference in the results of your campaign.

CHAPTER 21
Increase Response with a Follow-Up Kit and Conversion Series

The follow-up kit and conversion series are the critical final steps in your equity crowdfunding campaign to the investor.

They address this important, but sometimes overlooked question:

Once you have leads, then what?

Investors have responded, but they haven't made the final commitment to invest in your product or service.

That's where a follow-up kit and conversion series kick in.

First, the follow-up kit.

A follow-up kit is a package that can include multiple pieces, including a sales letter, magalog and additional value-added pieces.

I recommend sending the kit as both a hard copy and offering it as a link for download.

When I create a follow-up kit for a client, it includes powerful graphics to project a company's image and a strong cover letter using direct response copy to help convince the investor to respond.

A follow-up phone call after your prospect receives the kit will increase your shareholder conversion rate dramatically and should be part of any marketing plan.

Then, the conversion series kicks in.

A conversion series is a succession of emails, retargeting ads, pre-roll ads and postal letters that are independent of any phone calls by your sales people, complementing the sales process.

They follow leads to increase conversion and lead generation.

These are emails that I sent as part of a conversion series to prospects. Notice the first email tells prospects to watch for a magalog that they will receive in the mail. The second email follows up with prospects, asking them if they had received their free "magazine."

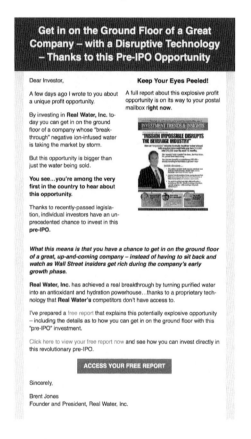

This conversion series may be expanded, as test results prove a longer series will continue to generate new investment funds.

After decades of seeing the amazing results of sending follow-up kits and using a conversion series, I encourage you never to skip this vital step in your marketing campaign.

Both of these elements can dramatically boost response and convert leads into buyers.

In fact, both the follow-up kit and conversion series will pay for themselves.

And remember, as with all the other critical components of your campaign, always follow the rules of direct response copy in your follow-up kit and conversion series.

CHAPTER 22
Analyzing Results to Improve Your Equity Crowdfunding Campaign

And finally: The results.

Along with testing and sending a follow-up kit and conversion series, you must analyze the results of your equity crowdfunding campaign.

This keeps your strategic marketing campaign accountable and it also helps you to continually refine your approach and learn what your audience will respond to.

With any kind of media that you produce, whether it be online or in print, you can determine the following two factors in testing:

1. The cost per lead
2. The cost per sale

For example, you can analyze your direct mail campaign so you know which lists worked and which did not, which teaser envelope copy worked and which did not – and any other test you may have performed.

I'm often asked, "What type of response can I expect?" Of course, all good marketers want to know how far their efforts will go.

This is impossible to answer since response is dependent on so many individual variables. Likewise, it's difficult to anticipate how many conversions will occur.

But the following can give you a guideline of realistic numbers of accredited investor leads you might get for 100,000 mailing pieces.

Accredited Investor Leads – 100,000 Mailing Pieces

Response Rate	Number of Leads	Cost per Lead (at a mailing cost of $1.00 per piece mailed)
.2	200	$500
.3	300	$333
.4	400	$250
.5	500	$200
.6	600	$167
.7	700	$143
.8	800	$125
.9	900	$111
1.0	1000	$100
1.1	1100	$91
1.2	1200	$83
1.3	1300	$77
1.4	1400	$71
1.5	1500	$67

Again, many variables impact your conversion. For example, if you have a conversion series of email and postal mail integrated with calls from a salesperson, that may significantly affect your results. Other factors include: if you're asking for $5,000, or asking for $100,000; how convincing and persuasive your salesperson is; and of course, how unique and exciting your offer is.

Below will give you a general idea of accredited investor conversions for 1,000 leads.

Conversion Rate of 1,000 Accredited Investor Leads

Conversion Percentage	Number of Investors	Funds Raised at $10,000 Per Investor
.2	2	$20,000
.5	5	$50,000
.8	8	$80,000
1	10	$100,000
2	20	$200,000
3	30	$300,000
4	40	$400,000
5	50	$500,000
6	60	$600,000
7	70	$700,000
8	80	$800,000
9	90	$900,000
10	100	$1,000,000

If your average investment is $100,000 or more, you can adjust the above accordingly.

Once you know how successful your campaign is, you continue your campaign according to the results. So, if you started with 100,000 mailing pieces and your goal was to get .8% lead rate, you go back to the winning versions and list cells and mail another 100,000, 150,000, 500,000 pieces. Just never mail more than the sales team can handle.

CHAPTER 23

Now What?

Marketing under the JOBS Act is a unique opportunity.

And it provides an even greater chance for success in raising capital for those who market in these early stages of equity crowdfunding.

Why?

Because right now, this marketing opportunity is new and your competition is almost nonexistent.

It takes time to begin a campaign and do it right.

My company, CDMG Inc., has pioneered the Investment Marketing field for more than 30 years, mixing human behavior science and big data.

I take a methodical approach to marketing that is different from branding or awareness, and targets investors directly and comprehensively.

These principles have generated billions of dollars in investments, Assets Under Management and shareholders for emerging companies.

So, here's what I suggest:

1. **Call Caleb Huey at (310) 212-5727 or email him at caleb@cdmginc.com.** Let's start a dialogue, discuss your goals and outline a strategic plan. If you would like, you are welcome to come to our offices in Torrance, California, or Nashville, Tennessee, and see our work, staff and 87 awards my team and I at Creative Direct Marketing Group have won for creating successful, winning campaigns.

 But if you can't visit us in person, that's okay. Over 75% of my clients have never been to our office.

2. **I can then send you a very tight proposal on the project: costs, strategy and schedule.** The good news: I will reduce your risk and help you succeed in raising capital.

I look forward to talking with you. Answering your questions. Helping you generate new capital. Creative Direct Marketing Group is here to help. So, give us a call at (310) 212-5727 or email Caleb at caleb@cdmginc.com.

What is an Accredited Investor? Keys for Marketing Under Regulation 506C

If you are marketing under Reg 506C, you'll be marketing exclusively to accredited investors.

As I explained in Chapter 3, I recommend that you market your investment offer under Reg A+. It is by far the best way to raise capital, and you can reach any investor regardless of income.

However, there are downsides to Reg A+. For example, it requires more money and paperwork to be able to qualify with the SEC.

In the case that you choose to market under Reg 506C, read on…

Keys to Success for Marketing Under Reg 506C

1. Know how to identify the accredited investor.
2. Know how to create a successful campaign to the accredited investor.
3. Know how to reach the accredited investor.

The first rule for marketing under 506C is knowing how to identify accredited investors.

So, what is an accredited investor? And how do you specifically reach this target group?

In Regulation D, Rule 506 of the Securities Act of 1933, an accredited investor is defined as any of the following:

(a) "An individual (or married couple) whose (joint) net worth exceeds $1 million, excluding the value of the primary residence;

(b) "An individual with income exceeding $200,000 in each

of the two most recent years, or a married couple with joint income exceeding $300,000 for those years, and a reasonable expectation of the same income level in the current year;

(c) "A bank, insurance company, registered investment company, business development company or small business investment company;

(d) "An employee benefit plan, within the meaning of the Employee Retirement Income Security Act (the benefit plan qualifies only if a bank, insurance company or registered investment adviser makes the investment decisions, or if the plan has total assets in excess of $5 million);

(e) "A charitable organization, corporation or partnership with assets exceeding $5 million;

(f) "A director, executive officer or general partner of the company selling the securities;

(g) "A business in which all the equity owners are accredited investors;

(h) "A trust with assets in excess of $5 million, not formed to acquire the securities offered, whose purchases a sophisticated person makes."

The estimated number of U.S. households that qualifies as accredited investors (based on net worth) is 10 million. That's 8.25% of all households!

As you can see, if you market under Reg 506C, you still have a large audience to reach. However, you've got to know how to reach them by knowing who they are, what they're interested in and what their spending habits are.

Investors and accredited investors are different – and respond differently to marketing tactics and strategies.

Accredited investors are a unique group of investors, besides being in the top 10% of all Americans.

For example, some are self-directed investors that prefer to be involved in all or most of their investment decisions.

And some rely totally or primarily on others for investment and financial information and advice. They use money managers or Registered Investment Professionals.

Many accredited investors are focused on personal financial issues because they enjoy being involved and active in their investments. And for others, their eyes glaze over if you talk about their finances or investments. They would much rather leave it up to the financial experts.

Some accredited investors are risk-averse and conservative. Others are risk-takers and aggressive with their investments – and everything in between.

They are not all the same. Their psychographics – how they behave based on their perceptions of reality and preferences – are just as important as their demographics.

Second, an integrated and multichannel campaign based on direct mail filtered data is the best choice to target the right audience of accredited investors.

I suggest that you follow all marketing recommendations I've made so far for Reg A+, including:
- A landing page
- Direct mail campaign
- Email marketing
- Banner ads
- Facebook ads
- Pre-roll ads
- Retargeting/look-a-like audiences
- Amazon ads
- Direct response video
- Conversion series
- Follow-up kit

The key for successful marketing under Reg 506C is to

target your integrated, multichannel campaign to accredited investors using names gathered from direct mail data.

By doing this, you'll effectively and accountably reach your target audience – and collect the leads you're looking for.

When your marketing is highly targeted, you'll see a reduction in cost and increase in profitability. This also speeds up the goal of raising capital.

Lastly, you'll need to know how to target accredited investors with direct mailing lists.

I have decades of experience in marketing to accredited investors with postal mailing lists. Companies like InfoMat know how to filter the right names.

If you are marketing under Reg 506C, you'll need to successfully target accredited investors with postal lists.

When combined with a multichannel, integrated campaign, this strategy will help you successfully raise the funds you need for your business or venture.

APPENDIX B:

A Massive New Opportunity for Investment Pools and Hedge Funds: Marketing Under the JOBS Act

It may be the case that you are not a business or company looking for investors, but an investment pool or hedge fund.

If that's the case, then the JOBS Act has changed the game for you.

Under the JOBS Act, equity crowdfunding is available for investment pools and hedge funds.

Never before has this been a possibility, but it's now a possibility.

Now, you can go directly to accredited investors when you market under Reg 506C to generate new assets under management.

Let me give you an example: For the Make America Great Again fund, I was able to create a direct mail campaign, an email campaign, a banner ad, retargeting campaign, landing page, conversion series and follow-up kit.

Marketing under the JOBS Act means you can generate investment capital in a new fund. Before, investors could only invest in a private company.

Not only are they investing privately in a fund, but they are investing in a fund that specializes in private companies.

Your investment fund can be any topic you want, targeting any investment-style you want. You now can market directly to the investor for it.

For the marketer of an investment pool or hedge fund, this is a huge opportunity to grow, expand and deliver profits. This change is not only beneficial to the investor, but to the investment "pros", who were previously restricted from communicating their investment philosophy and opportunity to the individual investor.

If you have an investment pool or hedge fund that you would like to market, I recommend that you follow the marketing plan outlined in the previous chapters, using the keys described in the next chapter.

APPENDIX C:
Equity Crowdfunding
Marketing Campaign Checklist

If you've read this book all the way through, you've received a lot of information, including multiple campaign elements and critical action steps to take.

Here's a checklist to help guide you step-by-step through developing and deploying your equity crowdfunding campaign:

1. **Develop a landing page.** First, you need to create a landing page created specifically for your investment opportunity. Follow the rules of direct response copy and make sure to include a powerful video on your landing page.

2. **Create a direct mail package.** A direct mail campaign targeted to investors will be one of your most powerful tools in your equity crowdfunding campaign. Depending on your investment opportunity, choose one of the recommended formats: traditional direct mail package, magalog, bookalog, 3-D package or videolog.

3. **Strategize for your email campaign.** Send direct response, plain text emails to the same names you have sent direct mail to, both before and after the direct mail arrives. Drive leads and new prospects to your landing page.

4. **Prospect and retarget with banner ads, Facebook ads, pre-roll ads and Amazon ads.** Create targeted ads to remarket your investment opportunity to existing prospects with custom lists, and to new prospects, using look-a-like audiences.

5. **Test, test, test.** Test all of your marketing efforts to improve your results. For example, perform A/B tests for email campaigns and banner ads to see which copy is more effective at generating leads...so that you can maximize results and profits.

6. **Follow up with a kit and conversion series.** Follow up leads with a kit of "special reports" or other value-added pieces. A personal phone call also produces amazing results. Create a conversion series of direct mail, email and ads that remarket your investment opportunity.

7. **Analyze the results.** Finally, test the results to see what worked and what didn't. Did you meet your goal? Analyzing results will allow you to choose the winning version, refine your approach and continue to improve your marketing campaign to investors.

APPENDIX D:

What You Should Know About Raising Capital Under Regulation CF

If it's the case that you are limited to marketing as Reg CF, you will be restricted in the following ways:

- How much capital you can raise ($1 million)
- What kinds of marketing and advertising you can engage in

The bottom line is this: if you plan on marketing your investment opportunity under Reg CF, you must use either a broker dealer or a crowdfunding portal to market your investment opportunity....and you can only raise up to $1 million in a 12-month period.

Here are some success stories from marketing under Reg CF:

- HelloMD is a health and wellness company that raised $1 million under Reg CF – and had to turn away an additional $700,000 from interested investors.
- Kylie.ai is an artificial intelligence company that raised $1 million through SeedInvest, a popular crowdfunding portal.
- BetaBionics raised $1 million to help fund its company that builds artificial pancreases for people with diabetes.

Over $55 million has been raised in total for Reg CF companies.

Crowdfunding portals can be an effective way to raise capital for smaller companies...

But the restrictions can outweigh the benefits.

For example, many companies do not reach their fundraising goal of $1 million in the correct amount of time (one year).

And you are restricted from advertising and marketing outside of your chosen crowdfunding portal.

Investors are also limited by how much money they can invest. Reg CF investors can invest the greater part of $2,200, or 5% of the lesser of their annual income or net worth, if their annual income or net worth is less than $107,000. If a Reg CF investor has an annual income or net worth of $107,000 or more, they may invest 10% of the lesser of their annual income or net worth.

JOBS Act Book NOTES

1) See "Jumpstart Our Business Startups Act," Wikipedia. Available at: https://en.wikipedia.org/wiki/Jumpstart_Our_Business_Startups_Act

2) See "JOBS Act and General Solicitation," American Landmark Properties. Available at: http://www.americanlandmark.com/learn-more/jobs-act-and-general-solicitation/

3) Miller, Zack, "Learn About Rewards-Based Crowdfunding," The Balance, 9 October 2017. Available at: https://www.thebalance.com/what-is-rewards-based-crowdfunding-985103

4) Miller, Zack, "Six Tools Used by Startup Investing Insiders to Identify – and Invest in – The Next Facebook," Forbes, 6 January 2014. Available at: https://www.forbes.com/sites/zackmiller/2014/01/06/6-tools-used-by-startup-investing-insiders-to-identify-and-invest-in-the-next-facebook/#2547626113ce

5) See "Total crowdfunding volume worldwide from 2012 to 2015 (in billion U.S. dollars)," Statista. Available at: https://www.statista.com/statistics/620952/total-crowdfunding-volume-worldwide/

6) See "Crowdfunding Industry Statistics," CrowdExpert.com. Available at: http://crowdexpert.com/crowdfunding-industry-statistics/

7) Chandran, Nyshka, "Equity crowdfunding gains traction in Asia," CNBC News, 9 November 2015. Available at: https://www.cnbc.com/2015/11/09/equity-crowdfunding-gains-traction-in-asia.html

8) Hogue, Joseph, "Crowdfunding 2018 Predictions: The Next Real Estate Boom?," Crowd 101, 1 December 2016. Available at: https://www.crowd101.com/crowdfunding-2016-predictions-the-next-real-estate-boom/

9) Alois, JD, "Virtuix Closes at $7.7 Million on SeedInvest Reg A+ Crowdfunding Offer," Crowdfund Insider, 1 August 2016. Available at: https://www.crowdfundinsider.com/2016/08/88637-virtuix-closes-7-7-million-seedinvest-reg-crowdfunding-offer/

10) Alois, JD, "Elio Motors Closes at $17 Million. Touts 50,000 Reservations," Crowdfund Insider, 4 February 2016. Available at: https://www.law360.com/articles/945348/celebrity-chef-bobby-flay-plans-15m-burger-palace-ipo https://www.crowdfundinsider.com/2016/02/81236-elio-motors-closes-at-17-million-touts-50000-reservations/

11) Alois, JD, "Chicken Soup for the Soul Entertainment Closes Reg A+ at $30 Million with Pre-Money Valuation of $120 Million," Crowdfund Insider, 17 August 2017. Available at: https://www.crowdfundinsider. com/2017/08/120781-chicken-soup-soul-entertainment-closes-reg-30-million-pre-money-valuation-120-million/

12) Alois, JD, "Adomani Closes Reg A+ Crowdfunding Offer at $14.4 Million. Next is Nasdaq Listing," Crowdfund Insider, 4 June 2017. Available at: https://www.crowdfundinsider.com/2017/06/101443-adomani-closes-reg-crowdfunding-offer-14-4-million-next-nasdaq-listing/

13) Hanson, Joyce, "Celebrity Chef Bobby Flay Plans $15M Burger Palace IPO, Law360. Available at: https://www.law360.com/articles/945348/ce-lebrity-chef-bobby-flay-plans-15m-burger-palace-ipo

14) Kaplan, Rob, Jr, "What's next in 2018? Growth in Reg A will bring new opportunities," HC Government, 8 Decemebr 2017. Available at: https://www.hcgovtrust.com/news-media/in-the-news/detail/2229/whats-next-in-2018-growth-in-reg-a-will-bring-new

15) Turner, Rod, "32 Companies Have Raised $396 mill of Capital Via Regulation A+ to Date; Details Here," Manhattan Street Capital, 29 March 2017. Available at: https://www.manhattanstreetcapital.com/blog/rod-turner/32-companies-have-raised-396-mill-capital-regulation-date-de-tails-here

16) Ibid.

17) Ibid.

18) Feldman, Amy, "Elio Motors, First Equity-Crowdfunded IPO, Soars Past $1B Valuation Days After Listing Shares," Forbes, 1 March 2016. Available at: https://www.forbes.com/sites/amyfeldman/2016/03/01/elio-motors-first-equity-crowdfunded-company-soars-past-1b-valuation-days-after-listing-shares/#728976d27844

19) Parker, Pete, "Equity Research Analyst's Stock Ratings: ADOMANO, Inc. (ADOM), Destination XL Group, Inc. (DXLG)," 11 October 2017. Available at: http://www.thewellesleysnews.com/2017/10/11/equity-re-search-analysts-stock-ratings-adomani-inc-adom-destination-xl-group-inc-dxlg/

20) See "ADOMANI Announces Initial Public Offering," Nasdaq Global Newswire, 15 June 2017. Available at: https://globenewswire.com/news-release/2017/06/15/1024865/0/en/ADOMANI-Announces-Initial-Public-Offering.html

21) Turner, Rod, "32 Companies Have Raised $396 mill of Capital Via Regulation A+ to Date; Details Here," Manhattan Street Capital, 29 March 2017. Available at: https://www.manhattanstreetcapital.com/blog/rod-turner/32-companies-have-raised-396-mill-capital-regulation-date-details-here

22) Ibid.

23) Morales, Sysy, "'Beta Bionics' Artificial Pancreas Company: First Startup to Raise $1 Million in Public Stock Option," Diabetes Daily. Available at: https://www.diabetesdaily.com/blog/beta-bionics-is-the-first-startup-to-raise-1-million-in-public-stock-option-297881/

24) Ibid.

25) Alois, JD, "Hops & Grain Hits $1 Million in Funding on Wefunder," Crowdfund Insider, 13 August 2016. Available at: https://www.crowdfundinsider.com/2016/08/89073-hops-grain-hits-1-million-funding-wefunder/

26) See "The Aspirational Class: How Many Accredited Investors Are There in America?," DQYDJ, 22 February 2018. Available at: https://dqydj.com/how-many-accredited-investors-are-there-in-america/

27) See "Case Studies," SeedInvest. Available at: https://www.seedinvest.com/case-studies

28) Ibid.

29) See "Beta Bionics," Wefunder. Available at: https://wefunder.com/beta.bionics

30) See "Stats at Wefunder," Wefunder. Available at: https://wefunder.com/stats

Book Index

110, 133

email, 16-20, 24-9, 31, 34, 37, 38, 45, 47, 50, 53, 62, 75-9, 88, 94, 98, 100, 110, 112-5, 117, 118, 121, 122, 126, 129, 130, 133, 135, 137, 138

envelope, 39, 47, 54, 59-63, 65, 70-72, 118, 125

equity crowdfunding campaign, 3, 22, 23, 29, 43, 46, 48, 49, 75, 78, 79, 81, 87, 91, 93, 95, 97, 98, 108, 115, 116, 121, 125, 137

Facebook, 16-19, 24, 25, 27-9, 34, 52, 53, 87-91, 94, 97, 99, 101, 102, 108-115, 117, 133, 137

Facebook ads, 16-9, 24, 27-9, 34, 52, 53, 88, 89, 91, 94, 109, 114, 115, 133, 137

follow-up kit, 28, 121-3, 125, 133, 135

Google, 28, 29, 81, 83, 93, 94, 99, 101, 103, 108

headline, 39, 42, 82-84, 90, 113, 118

highly targeted investor, 15, 71

InfoMat, 53, 134

Infomercials, 20, 109

Initial Public Offering/IPO, iii, 11, 12

integrated campaign, 17, 28, 29, 34, 75, 79, 97, 134

integrated marketing, 20, 23, 24, 26, 49, 52, 115

JOBS Act, iii, v, 1-5, 7, 9, 13, 16, 129, 135

lead generation, 28, 60, 62, 67, 68, 81, 91, 97, 122

lift note, 27, 59, 63, 72

list segmentation, 58

look-a-like audience, 18, 26, 81, 89, 94, 95, 99, 100-105, 107, 108, 115, 133, 137

magalog, 25, 27, 54, 59, 60, 65-67, 88, 121, 122, 137

mailing list, 17, 53-5, 70, 119, 134

mailing piece, 59, 71, 125-7

NASDAQ, 10, 11, 14

newsalog, 25, 27, 59, 67, 68

non-accredited investor, 12, 21

non-direct mail responsive, 57, 58, 146

paid search, 22, 37

Path #1, 15, 16, 19, 20-2, 33

Path #2, 19, 21, 22

Path #3, 21

pixel, 107, 108

plain text email, 76, 137

positive acceptance statement, 64, 70

PowerPoint, 48, 111

pre-roll commercials, 16, 18, 24, 27, 29, 34, 93-5, 97, 99, 101, 104, 115, 121, 133, 137

Real Water, 89

Regulation 506C, 7, 12-4, 56, 131, 131-5

Order Your Copy of
23 Equity Crowdfunding Secrets to Raising Capital

The Only Comprehensive Marketing Guide for Equity Crowdfunding, Written by America's #1 Authority on Marketing to Investors

First-Time Buyers Receive 20% Off…and a FREE Special Report

Order More Than One Book and Receive 30% Off…and a FREE Special Report

3 WAYS TO ORDER

Order on **Amazon.com** or on **www.equitycrowdfundingbook.com**

Order by phone at **(310) 212-5727**

Send this form to:
Creative Direct Marketing Agency,
Re: Craig Huey
21171 S. Western Ave.,
Suite 260, Torrance, CA 90501

✓ Yes! I want to learn how to effectively raise capital under the JOBS Act for my growing business. Please send me my discounted copy of *23 Equity Crowdfunding Secrets to Raising Capital* — plus my FREE special report on how to supercharge my marketing with direct mail.

TWO PURCHASING OPTIONS (CHECK ONE):

☐ **Save 20%.** Send me one copy of *23 Equity Crowdfunding Secrets to Raising Capital* – valued at $24.95 – for only $19.95, along with my FREE report, *12 Basic Rules for Successful Direct Mail Copy.*

OR

☐ **Save Up to 30%.** Send me _____ copies of *23 Equity Crowdfunding Secrets to Raising Capital* for only $16.95 per copy, along with my FREE report *12 Basic Rules for Successful Direct Mail Copy.*

METHOD OF PAYMENT:

_____Check or money order made out to **Creative Direct Marketing Agency**

Charge my: _____VISA _____MasterCard _____American Express

Name (as it appears on card) _____

Card Number _____

Exp Date _____ 3-4 Digit Security Code_____

Signature _____

Street Address _____

City, State, ZIP _____

Email_____Phone #_____

☐ Sign me up for *Direct Marketing Update* – Craig's weekly marketing newsletter on the latest marketing breakthroughs, plus concise tactics, case studies and test results all delivered directly to my inbox.

MAIL THIS FORM TO:

Creative Direct Marketing Agency, 21171 S. Western Ave., Suite 260 Torrance, CA 90501
Or, visit www.equitycrowdfundingbook.com to purchase a copy online today.

Dramatically Boost Sales, Leads and Profits with Accountable, Targeted Marketing

Nobody knows direct response and digital marketing better!

CREATIVE DIRECT MARKETING GROUP, INC. (CDMG) is a full-service, direct response advertising and digital marketing agency with one goal: increasing your response, market presence and profits through "accountable advertising."

Maximum response is achieved through over 40 years of experience in direct marketing including the use of thoroughly tested and responsive copy messaging, a comprehensive and multi-pronged delivery strategy and innovative yet cost-effective tactics.

At Creative Direct Marketing Agency, we build our campaigns on 4 powerful steps:

#1: Gain insight through extensive marketing research

#2: Enhance your ideas with driven creativity

#3: Build upon concepts with creative design and quality production

#4: Improve your long-term strategy with a complete analysis of your campaign

Using these powerful, time-tested steps we have helped turn entrepreneurial start-ups into large companies…and large companies into multibillion-dollar businesses.

If you're interested in hearing more about what we do… partnering with us to supercharge your marketing…or receiving a FREE critique from Craig, please do one or more of the following:

1 Give Craig a call at **(310) 212-5727** or email Caleb at **caleb@cdmginc.com.**

2 Visit us in our offices in Torrance, CA at 21171 S. Western Ave., Suite 260 Torrance, CA 90501, or in Nashville TN at 901 Woodland Street, Nashville, TN 37206. We'd love to meet you in person and show you around the offices.

3 Visit our webpage at **https://cdmginc.com** for powerful case studies, marketing insights you won't find anywhere else and video tutorials on how to supercharge your marketing.